The MOTHER-DAUGHTER Relationship Makeover

Workbook For Lasting Change

Companion Guide, Exercises, and Journal Prompts for The Mother-Daughter Relationship Makeover: Four Steps to Bring Back the Love by Leslie and Lindsey Glass. Companion Guide contributing author: Dee L. Fabry, Ph.D.

The MOTHER-DAUGHTER Relationship Makeover

Workbook for lasting change

Leslie and Lindsey Glass

Library of Congress Cataloging-in-Publication
Data is available through the Library of Congress

© 2025 Leslie Glass and Lindsey Glass
ISBN: 978-1-7324158-8-1 (Paperback)
ISBN: 979-8-218-81371-0 (ePub)

All rights reserved. Printed in the United States of America. No part of this publication may be reproduced, stored in a retrieval system, or transmitted in any form or by any means, electronic, mechanical, photocopying, recording, or otherwise, without the written permission of the publisher. Reach Out Recovery,

Cover, interior design and formatting by Haley LaFerney.

DISCLAIMER

The authors of **The Mother-Daughter Relationship Makeover (MDRM)** and its companion materials are not health care professionals. These materials are not intended to diagnose mental health disorders. We ourselves have done our recovery work by engaging with physicians, counselors, therapists, and other mental health professionals. We urge you to do the same.

CONTENTS

Acknowledgements · 9
Introduction · 11
Your Journey Begins · 13
Steps To Get Started · 15
Identifying Your Feelings · 17
Why Writing Is Important · 21

Step 1: Self-Discovery · 23
Leslie's Story & Lindsey's Story · 29
Emotional & Personality Styles · 33
Communication · 43
Getting Honest About the Secrets and Lies · 51

Step 2: Areas of Conflict: Food & Weight · 55
Finances & Money · 59
Appearance & Style · 63
Friends & Romantic Partners · 67
Dependence & Independence · 73
Boundaries & Detachment · 77
Alcohol & Drugs · 81
Mental Illness · 85

Step 3: Triggers, Trauma, & Conflict Resolution · 89
Trauma · 93
Techniques to Keep The Peace · 97
Breaking Up & Resources For Extreme Situations · 103

Step 4: Healing & Reconciliation · 107
Forgiveness & Healing · 111
Reconnecting With Purpose & Rekindling The Love · 115
The Recovery Lifestyle Coping & Resources For This Process · 119

Resources · 125
Praise · 127

ACKNOWLEDGEMENTS

To women everywhere who have inspired us with their stories, we thank you for your honesty, willingness to share your insights, and collaboration. We write for you. To all the reviewers, interviewers, journalists, podcasters, and radio hosts, who interviewed us during our six-month book tour for The Mother-Daughter Relationship Makeover: Four Steps to Heal The Love, thank you for your interest and enthusiastic participation.

Without the positive feedback, declarations of love for the book/process and encouragement to build this mother-daughter community, we never would have written this workbook, started our radio show on the Healthy Life Network, or begun work on our Mother Daughter seminar coming in 2026.

Our mother daughter work has grown due to the universal need for more understanding and tools to create lasting change. Thanks to Social Emotional Learning Professor, Dee Fabry PhD, for her insights and guidance and help in preparing this workbook. Thanks to Haley LaFerney who has worked with us for years designing our beautiful books and workbooks.

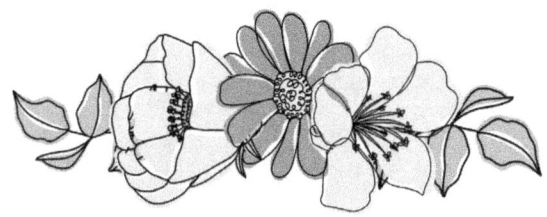

INTRODUCTION

Are you ready to set yourself up for success, not only in your mother/daughter relationship but in all your relationships? This workbook, based on the insights of the groundbreaking *Mother Daughter Relationship Makeover,* will empower you to achieve positive and lasting change and set you up for success. The key words here are ready, empower, change, and success. Let's start with change and recognize that every aspect of your life is changing all the time. Nothing stays the same except our profound longing for that one special love, our mom, or whoever mothered us.

Mom is our first, most enduring, passionate, and often turbulent relationship. You love her more than anything even when she's not perfect. Because of its intensity, however, and the many changes mothers and daughters experience over time, the mother/daughter relationship is especially vulnerable to bitter breakdowns. Your love feels thwarted, unrequited and it becomes difficult, if not impossible, to be together without fighting. Does that resonate with you? It's our story, too. As a mother and daughter who have experienced addiction, recovery, separation, bitter estrangement, forgiveness, and reconciliation, we know that life events can destroy any relationship, and positive change can happen only when we are ready to take control of what we think, what we feel, and how we behave.

EVERYONE IS RECOVERING FROM SOMETHING

It's a fact that everyone is recovering from something. Wherever you are in the world, or in life, you have experienced suffering and pain. Does everyone acknowledge old injuries and work to heal them? No, and what you don't know does hurt you. Some of your wounds are secret even from you. You may have been taught that everything was fine when your everyday life in childhood was far from fine. You may have been badly hurt by addiction or mental illness in a parent or friend. You may not have told anyone or even acknowledged who, or what, hurt you. Often, we don't recognize the whys of old feelings that cause problems in our relationships today. That's the reason we're here. What we feel may not be what really happened, so we need to investigate and maybe rethink our experiences to finally balance feeling with truth.

ARE YOU READY TO GROW

In every stage of life there is readiness: to walk, to learn, to achieve, to be happy, to overcome adversity, to thrive. If you're ready to reset your relationship with your mom/daughter, you are already empowered to see and say things you haven't said before, to think things you haven't considered before and to feel in ways that have not been open to you until now.

If you're reading this, you want to both explore the pitfalls that bedevil the precious mother-daughter relationship and find the tools you need to restore the love all mothers and daughters crave. Maybe you want a little information about what happened between you and receive hope that your relationship can improve. This workbook can give you answers, hope, and a lot more. The process that we have created for you here includes the steps that we took ourselves when we were heartbroken and thought our relationship could not be saved.

HOW WE GOT HERE

The short version of our story is that we are a mother and daughter who loved each other to the moon and back but could not get along. Although we worked together and had similar passions, we became toxic to each other and split up with no contact for four years. During that sad time, we both did a lot of work on ourselves; and finally we were able to find peace and reconcile.

Five years later we wrote a book about what happened and what we did to recover, *The Mother-Daughter Relationship Makeover Four Steps To Bring Back The Love*, by Leslie Glass – the mom – Lindsey Glass – the daughter. The wonderful reception to the book and the fact that it has been so widely recommended for therapeutic use led us to create a workbook to help people get everything they can from our four-step process. We could not be more excited to take you on this journey. Be excited. Be curious. This will be a transformational experience.

CHAPTER 1
YOUR JOURNEY BEGINS

You have chosen this book for a personal reason. Perhaps the title caught your attention. Maybe you are a mother struggling with how best to communicate and connect with your teenage or young adult daughter. Or you are a daughter frustrated with confusing messages from your mom. Whatever the reason, whatever your role, you are seeking guidance and direction.

You may be in counseling, therapy, or participating in some kind of professional help. Whatever your reason, you are ready to explore the mother-daughter relationship in some way. This workbook is written to help you in your recovery process, but it does not replace professional help. In fact, this may be a journey you want to take with a therapist or counselor, if you have one.

We share our mother-daughter stories to assure you that you are not alone in your struggle. As you read on, you may make a discovery that you are a lot like us. You will ask questions. You will get answers you may or may not like. It is hard and sometimes unsettling work, but it's worth the effort. If you need help, remember we did not do it alone.

Just like any journey that has the potential to change your life forever, we suggest that you make a commitment to yourself that you will keep at it to the end. Make the commitment in writing. Call it your contract with yourself. Research shows that when you take the time to thoughtfully agree to a process and write that agreement down, the greater the likelihood that you will do the work to create the change.

"NEVER UNDERESTIMATE THE POWER YOU HAVE TO TAKE YOUR LIFE IN A NEW DIRECTION."

-GERMANY KENT

CHAPTER 2
STEPS TO GET STARTED

1. Be sure you have a copy of *The Mother Daughter Relationship Makeover, Four Steps To Bring Back The Love,* By Leslie And Lindsey Glass. This is your reader's guide. Reading the book as you do the exercises will give you the background stories and research behind the exercises.

2. Choose Your Perfect Journal: It can be a spiral notebook or a blank journal whose cover you can decorate yourself. That's right! Give yourself permission to have some fun along the way. If you're crafty, you can make your journal a work of art as well as a tool for personal growth. You can use colored pens and pencils, create cards, book covers, drawings, collages, vision boards, whatever takes your fancy.

3. Open your journal to page one and **Create Your Contract** with yourself. Answer this prompt: *I am taking this self-discovery journey to . . .* Be truthful. No one else needs to ever see this journal. But the process of writing coupled with thinking and pondering allows time for your brain to make connections. It is through these connections and intersections that you can start the recovery process. Take all the time you need to state your intention and goals. When you feel that your agreement is complete, sign and date it. Your contract doesn't have to be long.

4. Get or make **Four Bookmarks** for easy access to your four sections. You can use ribbons or make fun bookmarks if you are crafty. The bookmarks and their title pages make your sections meaningful.

5. The first section in your journal is for **Journal Prompts.** This is a big section so give yourself many pages. Here you will write your answers to the questions we ask in each chapter. These journal prompts are important for several reasons. They will give you the information you need to add to your story. Your answers may change over time as you understand yourself better. That is the magic of personal growth.

6. The second section in your journal is for **My Personal Dictionary.** You can decorate the first page, or not. This section is your vocabulary builder and doesn't have to be too many pages. When you come across words or phrases that are new, make a note and take the time to increase your knowledge. We will include some words as we work through the book with you.

7. The third section in your journal is for **My Connections and Ideas.** Again you can decorate the title page or not. This is your section of "aha" moments. Give yourself some pages here if you like to take notes. When a thought, sentence, or idea makes you stop to think, quickly capture it in this section. Return to this section from time to time to explore your connections and ideas in-depth.

8. The fourth section in your journal is for **My Story.** This is where you take the answers from your journal prompts to write your own story. Not every chapter will invite you to add to your story, but you can add to it at any time, and keep it going after you have finished this workbook.

CHAPTER 3
IDENTIFYING YOUR FEELINGS

Feelings are the starting point of our journey because they are the key not only to the way we view the world, but also to the way we act, react, and manage our lives. For most of us, our thoughts and actions mirror our true feelings. Surprisingly, however, many people can't identify their feelings, where those feelings come from, or what to do with hurtful or destructive ones that cause problems in relationships.

In fact, for most of us a basic understanding of how to label, express, and manage feelings appropriately is very difficult. While toddlers are now taught to identify their feelings to help modify their behaviors, those lessons go out the window as students enter middle and high school where school culture is focused on academic achievement, not personal expression. It is in middle school that young people begin to hide their feelings to spare their parents and fit in with their peers. Furthermore, many adults today were never taught to think about their feelings in the first place. For these reasons most teens and adults have had little practice with identifying their emotions and managing them. As a consequence, negative feelings may spill out on a regular basis while positive feelings are not expressed.

WHAT ARE YOUR CORE FEELINGS

What feelings cause problems for you? You've heard of anger management, but that's just one on a spectrum of many negative emotions. No one needs happiness or gratitude management. Positive emotional and feeling states are what make relationships go smoothly and promote appreciation and love. And, they are just as important to identify as negative ones. Here's why.

Toddlers are taught the song, "If you're happy and you know it, clap your hands." As adults, when we're happy, we don't always know how to send messages of satisfaction and appreciation to our loved ones. "I love you. I honor and respect you. I'm proud of you," are examples of positive feelings that you may not be in the habit of expressing to your mom or grown children. "I really love it when you say or do…" is another example. Lindsey once sent Leslie a card that read, "You are my greatest earthly blessing." Leslie displayed it for 20 years. Even during their separation, that card was there to remind Leslie of a core feeling she hoped her daughter would recover.

So, while positive feelings and emotions don't need management, they may need help with identifying and expressing. Even more important, being aware of the impact of our negative feelings, thoughts, and actions, is crucial to having healthy relationships with loved ones, not only mothers and daughters. We can only do this work if we are clear and honest about how we feel and why.

To get a sense of where we are, we're going to jump right in with a quick self-assessment of feelings. We love assessments because we get to see where we started and how we progress.

FEELING YOUR FEELINGS AND WRITING ABOUT YOUR FEELINGS

Questions to think about. How do you and your mom/daughter feel and show your feelings? And what is the impact of those feelings on your relationship? But first, are you comfortable revealing your feelings on the page? If not, why not? Remember that only you will see this. Throughout this work, it is incredibly important for you to take the time to capture your thoughts in writing. Writing allows your brain time to make connections.

ADD TO YOUR DICTIONARY
Resentful
Wounded
Enraged
Grateful
Hopeful
Loving
Appreciative

QUICK FEELINGS CHECK EXERCISE

Can you rate how often you have each of these feelings everyday? Think about or write in your journal. Which feelings dominate your life?

FEELING:	NEVER	RARELY	SOMETIMES	USUALLY	ALWAYS
Angry – outraged, resentful, irritable, hostile, bellicose					
Sad – grief-stricken, gloomy, melancholic, despairing, hopeless					
Fearful – anxious, nervous, full of dread, concerned, skeptical, doubting, mistrusting					
Disgusted – contemptuous, revolted, disdainful, hateful					
Peaceful – tranquil, serene					
Enjoyment – happy, joyful, delighted, euphoric, Bliss, Gratification					
Loving – trusting, accepting, adoring, kind					
Positively surprised – thrilled, full of wonder, amazed, excited					

Identifying Your Feelings

DAILY MOOD TRACKER							
DATE:	Sun	Mon	Tues	Wed	Thur	Fri	Sat

HOURS SLEPT:

SLEEP QUALITY: 🙂 😐 🙁

ENERGY LEVEL: 🔋

TODAY I FEEL:
HAPPY JOYFUL GRATEFUL MOTIVATED
RELAXED RELIEF PROUD OPTIMISTIC
DEPRESSED ANXIETY DISGUSTED
HATEFUL SAD ANGER CONFUSED
INSECURE BORED LOST

MORNING MOOD:

AFTERNOON MOOD:

EVENING MOOD:

3 GOALS FOR TODAY:

3 THINGS I'M GRATEFUL FOR:

SELF-CARE:

WORKOUT MEDITATE BATH

SLEEP WELL NATURE TIME MUSIC

HEALTHY MEALS SHOPPING COOKING

READ A BOOK DO HOBBIES JOURNAL

PLAY GAMES LONG WALK FAMILY/FRIENDS

TV/MOVIES GRATITUDE

WHAT I ATE:

Breakfast:

Lunch:

Dinner:

Water Intake: ▯▯▯▯▯▯

DAILY JOURNAL ENTRY:

CHAPTER 4
WHY WRITING IS IMPORTANT

Reading assignment Chapter 1 of *The Mother Daughter Relationship Makeover* page 7

Writing has proven benefits especially in the area of self-reflection for personal growth. Writing, or journaling, can help you find clarity, manage uncomfortable emotions, and ease stress. For the purposes of this book, writing will also open the doors to self-discovery. Writing was a crucial part of our recovery because it helped us understand what went wrong, where our personality and communication patterns had become dysfunctional and how to think about what we wanted moving forward. We will ask you to write throughout this workbook because we know in those words will come the answers you're looking for to heal.

For those who have difficulty writing, you can record your answers to each of these questions. You will have an oral history of this journey. You can listen to your answers and see how you have changed over time.

Now that you have completed the feelings self-assessment, let's start our first journal prompts.

JOURNAL PROMPTS: FEELINGS

1. How are you with your feelings? Do you think they are generally under control or are they all over the place?

2. How was your mom with her feelings? Was she good or bad at expressing them?

3. Do you feel comfortable sharing your feelings with people? Be honest. This is where it's supposed to get a little uncomfortable. No one wants to think they deny themselves their feelings, but many do without realizing it.

4. Does your mom's or daughter's reactions to things make you afraid to tell her how you feel about things? Does she use guilt, denial, avoidance, or gaslight you, yell and scream?

5. Do you have any experience with journaling or tools to help clarify your feelings? Be bold and trust yourself. Again, if you want to talk into a recorder, speak your feelings out loud. It's just for you.

"WRITING IS TRANSFORMATIONAL BECAUSE IT TURNS A RANGE OF THOUGHTS AND EMOTIONS INTO A STORY WE CAN SEE, UNDERSTAND, AND LEARN FROM."

CHAPTER 5
STEP 1: SELF DISCOVERY

Reading Assignment: Chapter 2 of *The Mother Daughter Relationship Makeover* Page 13

Why do we think the way we do? Why do we do the things we do? Why do we keep behaving in ways that are no longer healthy? The answer may lie in the fact that we have not examined where our beliefs started, and why some of them stick with us even when they hurt us. So, where do our current beliefs and values come from? Our family or caregivers, of course. How do your family beliefs impact you? Who influenced your mother and father? Where did their beliefs come from? Have you ever analyzed or traced family and cultural values and beliefs? Is it time to do that?

WHO IS YOUR MOM

We begin with mom because she is literally your creator. How much do you really know about your mother, your grandmother, and all the women in your family's lineage? Many of us know very little about the events the women in our families have experienced. One of the things that was so fascinating about writing *The Mother-Daughter Relationship Makeover* was when Lindsey had to consider what her mom, Leslie, had been through. She had never considered what it had been like to be a mom in the seventies, long before most women had the support they really needed. What did her mom have to contend with in the working world at that time. What about the difficulties in her marriage?

In seriously considering and reading about her mother's life for this book, Lindsey realized her mom hadn't had it easy. In fact, she'd experienced many traumas of her own throughout her life. Being a mom without family around to help, having lost her own mom young was tough. That wasn't something Lindsey understood growing up. Lindsey had also never considered what it meant to be the mother of an addict. What was that like for her mom? These were new ideas to explore.

ADD TO YOUR DICTIONARY

Generational

Familial

Cultural

GETTING TO KNOW YOU

Who are you? This is the most important question we can ask. Interviewers for *The Mother Daughter Relationship Makeover* often asked us this question, and we were never sure what to include to adequately describe ourselves. Leslie is a mom, grandmom, mother in law; has been a daughter, author, cook, wife, philanthropist, author. Lindsey is a sister, sister-in-law, aunt, life coach, daughter, author, documentarian, screenwriter, content producer, loyal friend, dog mom. These labels of what we do may seem like enough to know us, but those lists don't begin to reveal who we really are.

LEARNING YOUR HISTORY

Self-discovery is the process of getting to know yourself. It can include many areas to explore but primarily starts with knowing your values, strengths, weaknesses, beliefs, and motivations. In this case, it also includes getting to know the history of your mom, daughter, grandmother, and all the women in your lineage. Self-discovery is influenced by generational trauma, experiences, and expectations.

What does this statement mean to you? "Your present conflicts develop from generational, familial, and cultural experiences." Have you ever considered that we are influenced by past generations and their beliefs and values? That we do things the way we do because we have never stopped to ask why.

On the mother's side, in reading Lindsey's story for the first time, Leslie realized many of the things Lindsey experienced were an exact mirror of her own history. That was a stunning revelation because she thought they were completely different. Leslie's compassion and understanding for what Lindsey went through as a young adult in recovery from addiction, and the extraordinarily gifted person she turned out to be, also grew from our own journey through this four-step process and writing the book. We didn't know each other until we learned about each other from our own telling of our stories. It's a gift we want to share.

Let's jump right into this process and start your brain thinking about what you know about yourself and the women in your lineage. Because, trust us when we say, the lifestyle, values, traditions, behaviors, habits, even the way we speak has been radically impacted by our mothers, the same is true for our mothers, and their mothers. If you have a well-documented line of healthy, independent, and confident women in your line, good for you! You are uncommon!

If you're like the rest of us, the females in your family have been impacted by a million different things including, immigration, discrimination, religion, class, looks, weight, ability to birth children, inability to birth children, alcoholism, mental illness, abuse, domestic violence, childhood trauma, rape, incest, bullying, or something else that scarred them along the way. Those things matter and sometimes need to be healed.

OUR INFLUENCERS FROM BIRTH

There are major traits to consider when you do this work. Every region in America and across the globe creates different habits and styles. If you grew up in one place, you will have the style and values of that place. If your family moved, they may have adopted the style and tastes of their new environment but still retain the values of former generations and countries. Unless your family has been in the same place for generations, your identity may have many components. Your mom or grandma may have immigrated or fled your country of origin. In addition, you most likely have a set of family traditions that are a mixture of cultural and generational influences. It is when we don't examine those influencers that our choices in life are controlled by traditions and history that have nothing to do with the way we live now.

CULTURE, CLASS, ETHNICITY, RELIGION

What's your mom's culture? What was her mom's culture? We all joke about the fiery Latina women or the icy Slavs but these stereotypes came about for a reason. We know there are truths to many cultures' habits around food and personality styles, which can be anything from overfeeding, to being controlling in all areas of their children's lives. Culture is a major factor that will influence the mother-daughter relationship.

Ethnicity is also a point of pride for some families and a source of fear and shame for others. We grew up in New York. In areas like Chinatown, Harlem, The Bronx, or Queens, with a polyglot of ethnic groups, it's easy to maintain cultural habits where there are many people like you. You see it in the food, the clothes, the stores, and ethnicity is unmistakable. Ethnicity, however, can become a giant source of conflict for mothers and daughters. Just think of all the issues that are rife with the potential to disagree: from marriage to friends to relatives to lifestyle choices, sexuality and even career choices.

Class and religion can also create strict guidelines for the way you behave, the clothes you wear, the amount you can spend, and the person you can date or marry. These are all big issues for mothers and daughters to fight about, and we see it everywhere from real life to TV and movies because this is the drama of real life. Are you going to follow your mom's wishes about religion and class? Did she follow her mom's wishes about those issues? Would you feel differently about your mom if you knew she was only repeating what she knew? Again, the fun of this chapter is beginning to reveal the story.

MENTAL HEALTH HISTORY & TRAUMA

Another result of self-discovery can be a game changer for everyone. Lindsey recently spoke to someone who was very angry at his mom. It came out that his mom had essentially been a child bride, married to an abusive alcoholic, and she had alcoholism and mental health issues herself. Even though she was not a great mom, once he understood what she had been through and the conditions under which she was trying to parent, he felt quite differently about her. Maybe you don't know that your grandmother was an alcoholic or depressive or that there is a long line of narcissists in your family. If you are someone who has anxiety, depression, addiction, it can well be genetic. It's a relief for many to find out that they "came by it honestly." It's a joke we think is funny. It means, you inherited something or learned it from your family.

Finding out what you can is helpful, especially if these are issues that are plaguing you or you are trying to heal from childhood abuse or family trauma.

Step 3 - Add key life events, which include abuse, trauma, divorce, separation, major medical issues, poverty, wars.

Step 4 - Choose your symbols and draw your genogram. Squares for men, circles for women, offspring can be diamonds, etc.

Free resource if needed https://creately.com/guides/mental-health-genogram/

LEARNING ACTIVITIES

"TURN YOUR WOUNDS INTO WISDOM"
-OPRAH WINFREY

Visual Collage - Create a collage with words, photos, drawings, and letters that describe your ethnicity, culture, class, and religion.

Mental Health Genogram - Draw your own, example below

WHAT IS A MENTAL HEALTH GENOGRAM

A mental health genogram is a helpful visual tool that maps your family's mental health history across multiple generations. It's different from a basic family tree, because it shows the patterns of mental illnesses, emotional dynamics, and recurring psychological traits. Mental health professionals use genograms to learn more about a person's background and history. Individuals can use genograms to shed light on how family history may be influencing their current mental well-being.

Step 1 - Gather family information going back at least two generations. Key family members and how they are related.

Step 2 - Identify mental health issues of family members (they don't have to have been diagnosed). If you noticed or heard someone talking about addiction, alcoholism, bipolar, depression, schizophrenia, eating disorders or anything else notable, mark it down.

EXAMPLE OF A MENTAL HEALTH GENOGRAM

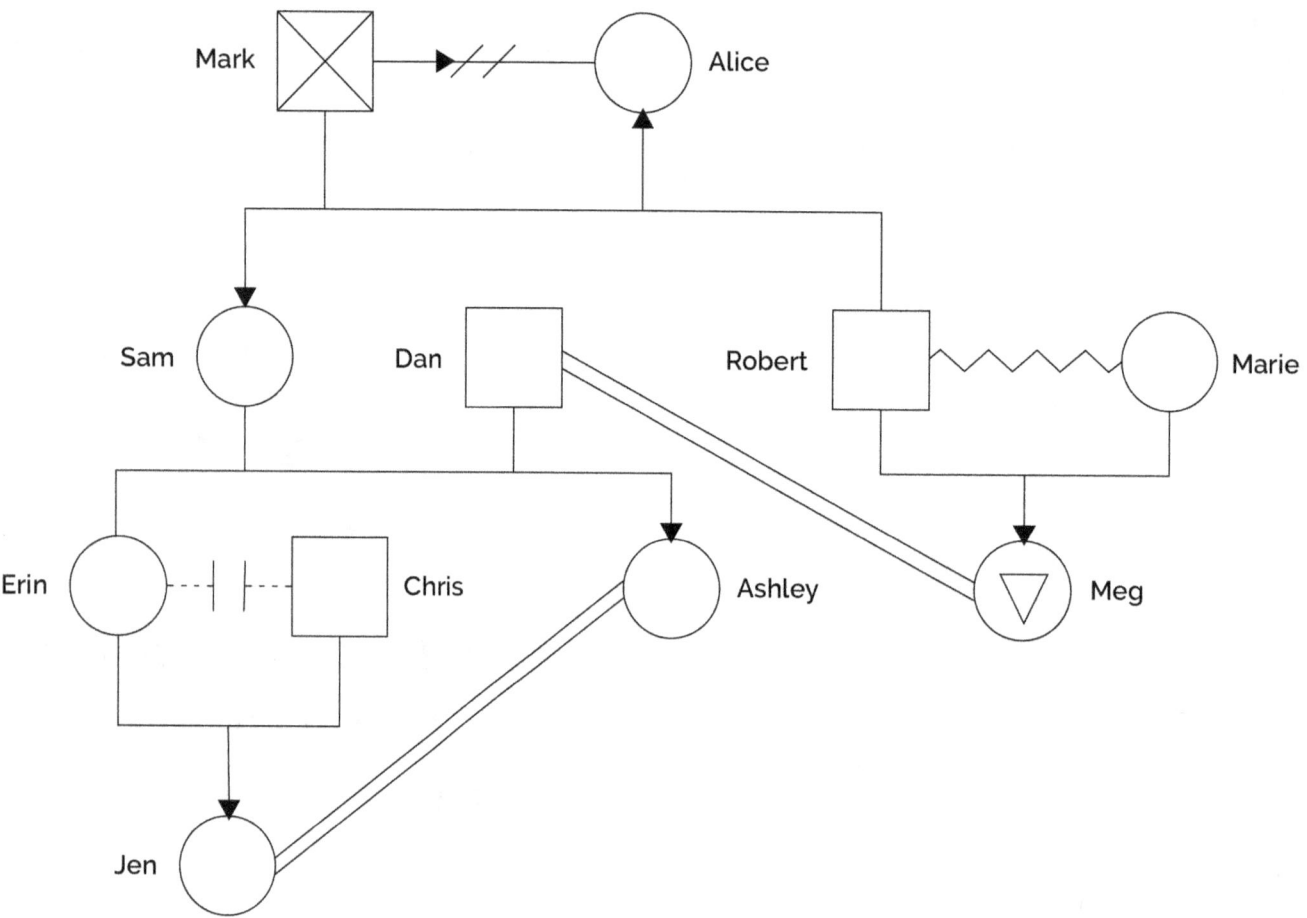

ASK YOUR MOM

Getting your mom's story is not always easy. We will be discussing secrets and lies in Chapter 5. Many moms and grandmoms don't want to share traumatic incidents and experiences that negatively impacted them. They may seem closed off and distant. To get to know your mom better, there are questions you can ask to help them to open up without feeling you're prying. These questions are non-judgemental and allow moms to share stories about pleasures, joys, and fun they might have had as children. Here are some examples.

10 QUESTIONS TO ASK YOUR MOM

1. What was your favorite game (toy, activity) as a child?
2. What were your favorite foods?
3. What did your mom teach you?
4. Did you have a favorite book?
5. What were your siblings like?
6. What was your favorite holiday and what did you do to celebrate?
7. What did you study at school, and what was your favorite subject?
8. Did you have pets or animals?
9. Did you live in the country or city? What was your favorite outfit?
10. What was the soundtrack of your childhood?

These are such basic questions, you may be surprised that you never thought of asking them. Moms generally like to be asked questions that don't put them on the spot. The journal prompts below will get you thinking about issues and challenges your mom and family might have faced that influenced generations before you and continue to influence you now.

Step 1: Self Discovery

If mom is not available, try asking an aunt, grandma, or anyone who may have memories of your childhood. If no witnesses of that time exists, you can create a story of what you would have liked for your childhood or what you would give your "inner child" now.

MY LIFE INFLUENCERS

Exploring Generational, Cultural, and Familial Influences. Who are the people who influenced you the most? Was it your grandmother with her country ways, or your aunt and uncle who were strict religious folk, or a depressed or alcoholic parent or sibling? Was your culture or ethnicity a big part of your upbringing or identity? What about your social class or religion? Here you can explore who or what had the most influence on your life.

JOURNAL PROMPTS: INFLUENCERS

1. What's your ethnicity? Did your family belong to any culture? Do you know where your family originally comes from?

2. Is/was your family religious? Was there conflict around religion in your home then or now? Were/are religious beliefs and traditions allowed to be discussed and questioned?

3. Do you know anything about your mom or grandmother's mental health history? Do you consider mental health an issue for you?

4. Is there any alcoholism, addiction, gambling, eating disorders, hoarding, or other addictions in the family? Do you struggle with any of these?

5. Are you aware of any trauma your mom/daughter or grandma may have experienced? Lost children, miscarriages, domestic violence, disease, war, etc.?

6. Have you ever talked to anyone about your own issues, whatever they might be? Was it helpful? What did you learn?

LIFE INFLUENCERS:	BORN DIED	ETHNICITY	RELIGION	MENTAL HEALTH	BEHAVIORAL ISSUES
MY MOM'S FAMILY					
Mother:					
Maternal Grandparents:					
Mom's Siblings: Aunts & Uncles					
MY DAD'S FAMILY					
Father:					
Paternal Grandparents:					
Dad's Siblings: Aunts & Uncles					
Me					
Sibling					
Sibling					
Sibling					

CHAPTER 6
LESLIE'S STORY & LINDSEY'S STORY

Reading Assignment: Chapter 2 of *The Mother Daughter Relationship Makeover* page 13

Everyone's story is different and interesting and special. You have elements in your story that are like no one else's. Your memories consist of so many different experiences: events, things people told you, relationship successes and failures, accomplishments, dreams you had that never came true, sad and hurtful incidents. We all have memories that shape who we are. As you write your story, you may remember things you didn't know mattered to you, like we did. You may see things in a different light at the end of the book, also like us. We wrote our story and were amazed at what was revealed.

To begin writing your own story, we're going to use ours as a model for you to see a variety of memories that you can include. Your story will reveal a lot about your relationship with your mom/daughter. Let's get to it.

YOUR BOOK REVIEW

As you read Lindsey's and Leslie's Story, what did you learn?

What major events in Leslie's life shaped her identity?

- When was she born?
- What were her father's beliefs about girls?
- What did Leslie know about her parents?
- What did her father do for a living?
- What were his barriers to success? Why?
- What was Leslie's mother like?
- What message did she send her daughter?
- What were the expectations of women during the time period 1945 – 1977?
- What was Leslie's schooling like?
- What was it like being a part of a very famous and influential family?

As you read about Leslie's *(the mother)* journey, how are you beginning to understand the multiple influences on a person? Make some notes about the way that Leslie's beliefs were formed and why. Who were the major influencers on her?

When Leslie shares her side of Lindsey's story what did you learn?

- What are the key things she shares about Lindsey?
- What does Lindsey feel were the most impactful events in her early years?
- What major events shaped Lindsey's identity?
- How did these challenges impact Lindsey's relationship with her mother?
- At what point did Lindsey split with her mother and why?

Take some time to pause and think about what you learned in **Chapter 2**. All relationships are complex, and the mother-daughter relationship is no exception. As you have learned, there are societal, cultural, ethnic, religious, class, and unexplored influences that help to shape a person. If we do not take the time to explore these factors, we cannot understand who we are and why we do the things we do. Now, pair that with the person who is responsible for you being here, the relationship is a minefield. Now is the time to tease out the components that shaped us.

- Religious beliefs (conservative or liberal, old fashioned or modern)
- Beliefs about women
- Did your mom or daughter have any wisdom to share

Keep this information in your journal as we continue our discovery process, and you develop your story. Answer the following journal prompts and then begin to write your story.

LEARNING ACTIVITIES

JOURNAL PROMPTS : YOUR STORY

1. In a couple of paragraphs tell your mother's story. Who is she; where did she come from? What was her life like? How was she as a mom?

2. In a couple of paragraphs, tell your story. Who are you? Where did you come from? What was your life like growing up?

3. Describe a history of your relationship with your mom or daughter.

4. What is your relationship with your mom or daughter now?

5. What about your mom/daughter makes you mad, sad, unhappy?

6. What about your mom/daughter makes you smile, be proud, and happy?

7. How would you like your relationship with your mom/daughter to be different?

TIPS FOR TELLING YOUR STORY

Hints on how to tell your backstory - how to reveal and flesh out your own story.

Accessing Your Memories

- What helps you remember
- Smells
- Foods
- Music
- Geography - summers, vacations
- Transportation
- Chores
- Attitude about school, friends
- Things that made you happy
- Things you did with your mom
- Things you did with your daughter
- What were your cultural traditions

"THE MORE A DAUGHTER KNOWS THE DETAILS OF HER MOTHER'S LIFE... THE STRONGER THE DAUGHTER."

—ANITA DIAMANT
THE RED TENT

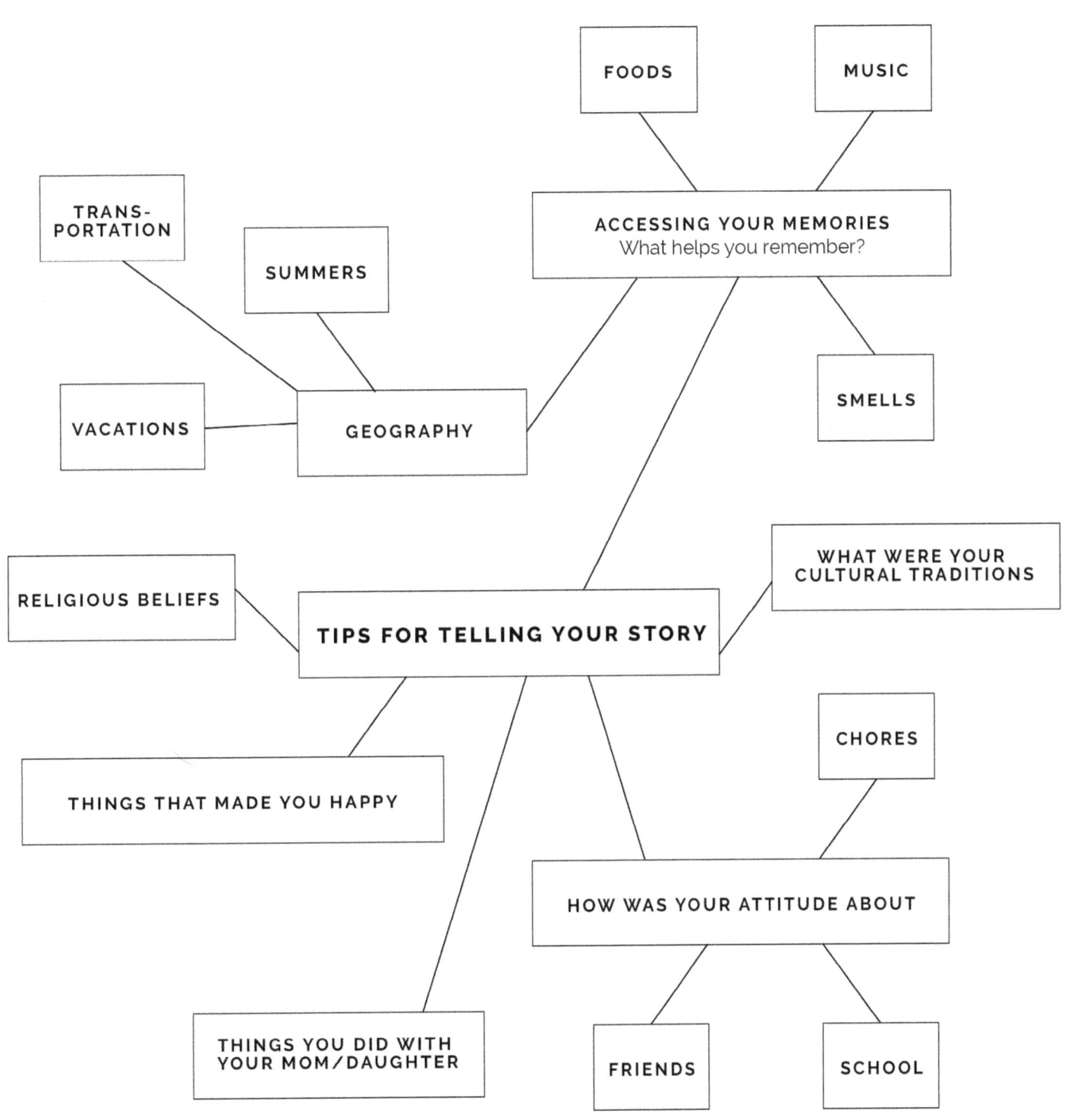

CHAPTER 7
EMOTIONAL & PERSONALITY STYLES

Reading Assignment: Chapter 3 of *The Mother Daughter Relationship Makeover* Page 43

Your mom's and your emotional and personality styles have impacted your relationship from the very moment you were born. What if you're a great match, and what if you're not? Remember, your mom's situation when you were born as well as many other factors influenced the way she interacted and treated you. Loving, neglectful, sad, distracted, anxious, joyous? And you influenced her as well.

What were you like as a baby, child, teen, young adult? Many babies are fussy, demanding, unable to settle down. Happy babies make happy moms, and by the same token unhappy moms can create anxious and fearful children. Yes, even babies can be depressed. Imagine how you would feel if you spent nine months inside someone who was angry and not caring for her body the way she should be preparing for a healthy baby, or taking care of herself after you were born. Many pregnant women and new moms find themselves in hard or stressful circumstances.

UNPACKING YOUR RELATIONSHIP PACKAGE

Circumstances are only one piece of your relationship puzzle. Have you ever thought about your mom's personality traits and her moods? Are they different from yours? You may be very much alike and get along like perfect peas in a pod. But you may be different in ways that you never considered. Conflicting personality and emotional styles can cause a lifetime of drama if you don't understand your other person and the most effective ways to communicate with her. We know plenty of families coping with difficult or depressed moms and daughters whose moods, rage, and instability make life challenging at best. Emotional and personality styles of both moms and daughters are many, and they change over time.

What we love about this part of self-discovery is that it immediately sheds light on your relationship situation. We know that with new-found clarity you will find solutions you didn't think were possible.

MOOD MATTERS

Before we dive into personality traits, let's return to emotions for a moment. We talked about feelings, and feelings are one component of your emotional style or emotional inner life. Where are you with your emotions? Do you feel dead inside and struggle to feel your emotions, or are they all over the place and often out of control? Sometimes, we can hardly keep up with how many times our moods change in a day.

By the way, age and hormones play a huge role in women's physical and mental wellbeing in our stages of development and throughout our lives. Hormones can be our worst enemy and often at the most inconvenient times, as in the teen years, around pregnancy and childbirth, when we hit our mid forties or fifties. Hormones are a plague on many women who are already struggling to understand and manage emotions. 'Brain on fire' is an accurate term for the havoc hormones inflict on us just when we need stability most. Also, what are your mood habits? Do you often reset into a negative mood or are you good at staying positive? You might make a note to think about this in preparation for the journal prompts at the end of the chapter.

MOOD METER: HOW ARE YOU FEELING?									
Enraged	Panicked	Stressed	Jittery	Shocked	Surprised	Upbeat	Festive	Exhilarated	Ecstatic
Livid	Furious	Frustrated	Tense	Stunned	Hyper	Cheerful	Motivated	inspired	Elated
Fuming	Frightened	Angry	Nervous	Restless	Energized	Lively	Enthusiastic	Optimistic	Excited
Anxious	Apprehensive	Worried	Irritated	Annoyed	Pleased	Happy	Focused	Proud	Thrilled
Repulsed	Troubled	Concerned	Uneasy	Peeved	Pleasant	Joyful	Hopeful	Playful	Blissful
Disgusted	Glum	Disappointed	Down	Apathetic	At Ease	Easygoing	Content	Loving	Fulfilled
Pessimistic	Morose	Discouraged	Sad	Bored	Calm	Secure	Satisfied	Grateful	Touched
Alienated	Miserable	Lonely	Disheartened	Tired	Relaxed	Chill	Restful	Blessed	Balanced
Despondent	Depressed	Sullen	Exhausted	Fatigued	Mellow	Thoughtful	Peaceful	Comfy	Carefree
Despair	Hopeless	Desolate	Spent	Drained	Sleepy	Complacent	Tranquil	Cozy	Serene

↑ ENERGY ← SPECTRUM →

PERSONALITY STYLES

You have a personality style; do you know what it is? In other words, do you have a strong understanding of who you are and how your behavior looks to others? When we started writing this book, Leslie thought Lindsey was the most controlling person on earth, and Lindsey thought Leslie was the most controlling person on earth. That was an astounding revelation. When we read each other's chapters on personality, we realized that we don't see ourselves as others see us. Same with conflict. We both thought of ourselves as conflict averse and the other as the argument-seeking party. In short, we both saw ourselves as nicer and more reasonable than we appeared to the other.

See how personalities and traits can get confusing in a dynamic like this? Sometimes it is helpful to step back and investigate further to attain more information about what's really going on. Investigating may include asking a relative whose opinion you can trust. What am I really like? Am I being mean? Is mom controlling? These are questions you might consider asking. We rarely see ourselves the way other people see us, and we definitely don't see ourselves when we're in conflict and not behaving our best.

Here's the truth. Some mothers are nicer to their pets than to their children, or seem like wonderful people at work and in the world but are tyrants at home. The same goes for daughters. Some are delightful, cheerful creatures, and some can be mean as snakes to their mothers, constantly criticizing or making them feel bad. On the other side, we have the pushovers, the people-pleasers, and the mothers and daughters who can't stand up for themselves and suffer in silence.

Learning what kind of personality and emotional style you and your mother have may come as a complete surprise. But, the goal is to provide clarity. Finding out that a mom who wasn't emotional really wasn't capable of showing much emotion because of her upbringing or personality makeup can be life-changing. Or to know that a mom with no backbone was really a passive or melancholic personality might give you more compassion for them. It did for us.

First, let's explore a few emotional styles of moms and daughters as you discover your own in this chapter. These 'types' are just tools to help you better understand yourself and your mom. Make notes in these charts as you read.

HIPPOCRATES FOUR TEMPERAMENTS

There's a long history of philosophers trying to explain and describe the reasons behind human behavior. The study of personality can be said to have its origins in the fundamental idea that people are distinguished by their characteristics. Over time, many eras produced thinkers who invented, explained, and interpreted theories about the different types of behavior people are born with, or develop. We will start, however, with the very first theory that traces back more than 2,000 years and was conceived by Hippocrates in ancient Greece. While Hippocrates' temperaments were based on long-outdated ideas about blood humors influencing attitudes, we still refer to his four temperaments to this day. Let's explore.

Sanguine: Sanguine comes from the Latin word for blood, and a ruddy complexion was viewed as hearty, positive and optimistic. Other synonyms for your emotions dictionary include hopeful, confident, cheerful, buoyant, assured. These days the sanguine personality might include social usefulness, someone who is active and great in communities like church or your sorority, team, or work group.

Choleric: The actual meaning of choleric is someone who is easily moved to often unreasonable or excessive anger, in other words, hot-tempered as in a perpetually choleric old grouser. Know any of those? This type can be an arrogant person who has a high opinion of him/herself. The description of the choleric personality these days is more generous, along the lines of quick-thinking, influential, competitive, independent, easily annoyed, prideful, and with leadership qualities. There can also be an element of narcissism in this personality type. While narcissists may be choleric, not all cholerics are narcissists.

Melancholic: According to the Greeks, this meant too much black bile. Hence the term melancholic is associated with a feeling of sadness without specific cause and has a connotation of brooding and reserved. On the positive side, people with a melancholic temperament tend to be perfectionists, artists, creative and deep thinkers. They can be sensitive, empathetic, reserved and often quiet. The melancholic personality type can appear dark, depressed, detail-oriented, and calm, but with intense emotions. On the positive side, traits also include dependability, task-oriented, empathic and loyal.

Phlegmatic: This type was diagnosed in Greek times as having too much phlegm, a humor which made this personality category slow and easygoing. You could also say lazy and laid back. While the other three temperaments are prone to being high-strung, excitable, perfectionist, and highly motivated, they could take a lesson from the phlegmatic type in how to take life slow and steady, with contentedness. The phlegmatic personality is calm, reliable and the easiest to get along with as long as you have the patience to explain and elaborate, because phlegmatics take time to process.

Rate Yourself By Hippocates Description:

TYPE	DESCRIPTION	MOM	DAUGHTER
Sanguine	Optimistic, Social		
Choleric	Extroverted, Competitive		
Melancholic	Analytical, Loyal, Empathic		
Phlegmatic	Relaxed, Easy going		

"PARENTING IS ABOUT RAISING AND CELEBRATING THE CHILD YOU HAVE, NOT THE CHILD YOU THOUGHT YOU'D HAVE."
-BRENE BROWN

JOHNS HOPKINS FOUR PERSONALITY TYPES

Over the years other personality definitions have been created. The most recent was developed according to a Johns Hopkins study based on the traits of open-mindedness, extraversion, neuroticism, agreeableness, and conscientiousness. Again, four basic personality types are defined: Average, Reserved, Self-Centered, Role Model.

Average: This type is defined as people who are high in neuroticism (a tendency toward negative emotions including anxiety, depression, and volatility) as well as being low in open-mindedness. At the same time the average person, while harboring self-doubt, may appear social and outgoing, even self-confident. Most people fall into this category, which is also characterized by being opinionated and closed-minded. Are you surprised to hear that women often fit into this category? Do you recognize the duality of being anxious yet social, full of self-doubt yet appearing self-confident? Keep in mind the close-minded quality you may recognize in yourself or your mom/daughter. This is where we want to change a habit that doesn't serve you. It's when you open your mind to new ideas that you also open your heart to love, compassion, and forgiveness.

Reserved: This type is defined as people who are high in agreeableness and low in extraversion and neuroticism. You know the type. Quiet, often polite and thoughtful, but not very outgoing. Reserved people often prefer their own company, and you may never know what they are really thinking and feeling.

Self-centered: This type is defined as people who are high in extraversion, yet below average in openness, agreeableness, and conscientiousness. The size of this population typically increases with age. Self-centered people are the ones who dominate conversations, share all their opinions about everything, and want and expect things to go their way. Self-centered people don't see other people's points of view.

Role model: This type is defined as those who are low in neuroticism and high on open-mindedness, extraversion, agreeableness, and conscientiousness. Apparently, this is the group you want to be associated with. They can see other people's perspectives and are empathetic and fair. They often have a high level of emotional self-awareness.

When you think about your own personality, where does it fall? Are you neurotic or a touch paranoid always worried about what's going to happen next? That can also be a red flag for an anxiety disorder. Are you an introvert who hates dealing with people, places, and things? We know plenty of those, and it's always wild to see a mom and daughter where one is an introvert, and one is an extrovert and rarely do they want to do the same thing. It happens more often than you think.

Then, on the opposite end of the personality spectrum, you have the self-centered and the role model. Where's your mom or daughter in that mix? When it comes to moms and daughters, you can be a mix, or different at different times in your life. Remember, who your mom was at 25 is not who she was at 45 or 65. Same for you.

With Leslie and Lindsey, what's wonderful about our relationship now is that we are both radically different people from who we were decades ago, before Lindsey was sober when she was still facing some of her own demons and Leslie was desperately trying to "save" her. We'd both agree that in those years we could be selfish, inconsiderate, neurotic, and more. But, with time and understanding of how those behaviors affected each other, we were willing to change. Let's see what you uncover and what you're willing to change!

Rate Yourself By Johns Hopkins Personality Types

TYPE	DESCRIPTION	MOM	DAUGHTER
Average	Tend to have negative emotions, are neurotic, anxious, volatile, closed-minded, social yet self-doubting		
Reserved	Highly agreeable, quiet, polite, not outgoing, not easy to read.		
Self-Centered	Dominating, opinionated, self-centered, has to be right		
Role Model	Empathic, fair, self-aware, conscientious, extroverted, agreeable		

Emotional & Personality Styles

YOUR DAUGHTER'S PERSONALITY STYLE

Do you look at your daughter and wonder where she comes from? Daughters can be wildly different from their moms, and it's quite the shock when it happens to you. Many moms, including Lindsey's, have wondered, "Where did this pink-haired creature in ripped jeans come from? She's definitely not mine!" Daughters can be all over the map so let's see where your daughter falls.

Here is another way to define your daughter's personality style.

TYPE	DESCRIPTION	MOM	DAUGHTER
Rebel	In trouble, rule breaker		
Easygoing	Very adaptable and gets along with everyone		
Peacemaker	Dislikes confrontation		
Family clown	Funny and entertaining, insecure		
Quiet	Feels invisible, sensitive		
Loud	Confident or bossy		
Caretaker	Selfless, helpful		
People pleaser	Do anything to please others		
Manipulator	Loves to push buttons		
Sneaky	Great liar, hides what is going on		

YOUR MOM'S PARENTING STYLE

We all know moms can be all over the map with their parenting styles. We see them in real life, on TV, in the movies, and they are all recognizable. So, what is your mom's parenting style? Is/was she emotionally available, or not so much? Was she the life of the party or a total drama queen? Did her every emotion dictate her parenting choices? Now is the time to break it down.

TYPE	DESCRIPTION	MOM	DAUGHTER
Cool & detached	Distant and not emotionally available		
Roller coaster	Fun and irresponsible		
Hysteric & anxious	Drama queen		
Empathic	Aware of your moods and wants you to feel better/co-dependent		
Perfectionist, self-righteous know-it-all	Knows it all		
Balanced	Emotionally mature		

ADD TO YOUR DICTIONARY

Sanguine

Choleric

Melancholic

Phlegmatic

Self-Centered

Self-Aware

CONNECTING THE DOTS: PERSONALITY AND EMOTIONAL INTELLIGENCE

There's another component of emotional styles that we are going to add here. In this chapter we've been exploring personality traits which are related to behavior to others. We've talked about moods and feelings. Now we're going to add another kind of measurement. To reveal who we are and how we affect others, we're going to connect the dots between personality, emotions, and emotional intelligence. And there's nothing artificial about this kind of intelligence.

EQ OR EMOTIONAL INTELLIGENCE

Emotional intelligence is the ability to recognize, understand, and manage moods, emotions, motivations and interactions with others. Let's explain. In school and at home, children are often judged by their behavior and academic achievements. Academic achievement and good behavior, however, are not necessarily indicators of emotional health, which include good communication skills, caring for others, drive, problem-solving, self-management (including mood, food, and habits), and self-esteem which are the qualities most needed for healthy relationships.

What's the difference between your EQ and your IQ? First, what do IQ, or intelligence tests really tell us? Frankly, they're limited, like the labels we give ourselves, and others. IQ tests measure cognitive functioning, including verbal, mathematical, visuospatial reasoning, memory, attention, and language comprehension.

A high IQ means you could be a brain surgeon or a rocket scientist. Students who don't do well on IQ tests may think they're stupid, but actually may have other important qualities that bring them great success in life. You don't actually have to have a high IQ to be smart or to be successful.

So what is your EQ or emotional intelligence, and why does it matter? Your EQ is the part of brain function that brings heart and purpose to your thoughts and actions. That's a metaphor. Your heart is just a pump and can't think. Your brain is the computer that runs the whole show, your body and your mind. We'll talk a lot more about the brain later. But while you may not have the academic ability to be a rocket scientist, your emotional intelligence is the part of your brain that can be trained and improved. Below is a chart with some components of EQ.

A FEW WORDS ON SOCIAL AND EMOTIONAL LEARNING (SEL)

Social and emotional learning is an essential part of human development. What is social and emotional learning? According to the Collaborative for Academic, Social, and Emotional Learning (CASEL) (CASEL.org) social and emotional learning (SEL) is the process that all people acquire knowledge, skills, and attitudes to develop healthy identities, manage emotions, set and achieve personal and collective goals, feel and show empathy for others, establish and maintain supportive, trusting relationships, and make responsible and caring decisions. SEL growth is a lifelong process as we develop ever increasingly effective skills. **The five key components of SEL are:** self-awareness, self-management or self-regulation, social awareness, relationship skills, and responsible decision-making.

You are exploring the impact of social and emotional competencies on your mother-daughter relationship in this book. Unfortunately, not everyone is taught effective SEL knowledge and skills during their childhoods and adolescent years. You may be experiencing the results of 'not knowing what you don't know."

The following four SEL competencies impact your ability to have healthy relationships and make more effective decisions. We never stop increasing our SEL knowledge and skills – unless we stop learning and growing.

Self-awareness, which is the ability to accurately identify emotions in yourself and others. You must first be able to accurately name and express your emotions before you can begin to manage them.

Self-management or self-regulation is the ability to control our reactions and responses to life's situations. Learning how to use breath control to slow your reactions, how to allow time for the brain to process information, and how to make better choices are all part of self-regulation. Those are all learned skills.

Social awareness is paying attention to the reactions and feelings of others and learning to not make critical judgments. Having an open mindset allows for better understanding.

Relationship management is all about communicating effectively, compromising, and collaborating to make relationships run smoothly and satisfactorily for everyone.

SELF-AWARENESS: HOW AWARE ARE YOU OF YOUR FEELINGS

Let's explore EQ with some real life examples.
When Lindsey went into rehab at 21, she struggled to adequately describe her feelings. She wasn't used to paying attention to what she felt in her body, what it meant, as well as how to respond in an emotionally appropriate way. Maybe you're someone who has deep self-awareness and you know how to care for yourself, but maybe this is all new to you and learning a vocabulary to talk about your feelings will be very helpful.

SELF AWARENESS EXAMPLES

Whenever anyone asks Lucy a question, she gets defensive and starts yelling. The people she yells at always respond in kind, and fights ensue. Lucy fights with everyone. Here's one reason. Lucy is very sensitive to criticism and thinks everyone is out to get her. What's behind Lucy's sensitivity and response? Her mother, Mindy, the lawyer, has always used questions to put Lucy on the defensive about everything she says and does.

"Why do you do this? Why do you do that?" Because Lucy's mom asks pointed questions that imply she's doing something wrong, Lucy interprets even the simplest, most normal and neutral questions as personal attacks. Mindy doesn't have the self-awareness to understand that questioning her daughter like a litigation lawyer has created a daughter with hypervigilance and acute sensitivity to criticism.

Lindsey learned the expression HALT in recovery. When you feel Hungry, Angry, Lonely, or Tired, all kinds of bad things can happen. Becoming self-aware around both physical and emotional needs, means that you can manage your physical health as well as potentially negative and hostile interactions with other people. Learning how being hungry, angry, tired or lonely affected her relationships, Lindsey was able to ensure that she gets enough sleep, always has a snack and water on hand, and can take a break to sort herself out whenever she's caught off guard emotionally.

SELF-MANAGEMENT: HOW IS YOUR SELF-CONTROL

Self-management is also self-regulation (and self-control) and has a number of components. In emotional terms, it would apply to motivation to do better, to have an open mind and desire to learn more. The ability to develop and improve is part of self-management. But it's also related to the ability to control your moods and know when to stop an unhealthy habit or activity, and be able to communicate in a healthy way.

SELF-MANAGEMENT EXAMPLES

Morgan is a testy teen. She's moody, doesn't do chores, has outbursts at the dinner table. It's hard to get her to clean her room. She doesn't make her bed. Sometimes she eats too much, and sometimes she starves herself. Morgan skips school and homework whenever she feels like it. Morgan is a handful and seems never to have a happy moment. It's not uncommon for teens with raging hormones to have difficulty with self-regulation, getting on track and staying on track. But what is really going on with this particular teen? Moms need to understand their part in their teens' emotional life. Allison is Morgan's mom, she is the queen of self management. Everything in her world has to be perfect. She speaks three languages, cooks to perfection, manages the budget, has a demanding job, and is constantly nagging Morgan to get with it or else some dire, terrible thing is going to happen to them all. Morgan won't get into college. She'll be too fat to fit into any prom dress. She'll never be a good wife, or even get a boyfriend or husband. Allison is a catastrophizer, and she is particularly resentful because Morgan often has her outbursts during dinner after Allison has made an effort to serve a great meal, thus disrupting family time and ruining her mom's sense of competency.

Two things, and a lot of conflict, are at work here. Morgan is going through tough teen years, and mom is only looking at behavior and not what Morgan is feeling or why she's rebelling. While Allison has great self-management skills for herself, she is lacking in self-awareness of how she appears to her daughter, and this mom has no self-control with regard to beating her daughter up for what she perceives are Morgan's shortcomings. So Morgan is rebelling, and Allison is controlling without being supportive. For Morgan to change, Allison needs to understand how she seems as a mom.

SOCIAL AWARENESS: CAN YOU READ THE FEELINGS OF OTHERS

This is a sensitivity question and goes right along with self-awareness and self-control. One of the most important components of EQ is empathy which includes compassion. Are you the empath type who sees and feels all and is almost unable to keep others' feelings and reactions from affecting you? Or are you the type who barely notices how other people see you and acts however you want despite people's reactions? Being able to read other people is a skill, but some moms and daughters are better and more intuitive and thoughtful than others.

SOCIAL AWARENESS EXAMPLES

Geraldine is a mom who dresses outrageously, drinks a lot, and tries to join her daughter, Eloise's get-togethers with her friends. Eloise is constantly embarrassed and humiliated by her mom's lack of boundaries and antics. Geraldine joins in where she's not welcome and doesn't see how exasperated and annoyed her daughter is. She just can't read the room and calm down. Do you have a mom like this?

Grace is an adult daughter who is dismissive of her mom's efforts to help with the children. She doesn't think her mom, Jane, a mother of four successful adults, knows how to change a diaper or feed a toddler. Grace criticizes her mom's choice of clothes, saying she looks frumpy and fat despite the hurt look on her mom's face. Grace thinks Jane is out of step with the times and lets her know it. Do you have a daughter like this? Why would a daughter act like this?

On the other end of the spectrum is Carolyn, a mom with great social awareness. When Carolyn's shy daughter, Marly, cringes at something she said, Carolyn immediately rescues the situation by backtracking or changing the subject. Her message to Marly (and everyone else she knows) is "I'm watching. I know how you feel. I've got your back."

SENSITIVITY TO CONTEXT: HOW GOOD ARE YOU AT ADAPTING

Following up on how our sensitivity can bring us to our knees, what about your ability to pivot and not be overwhelmed by negative situations? Here, we're talking about instant hurt feelings when we think we're being challenged or insulted. All of us want to believe that we're good people; we're competent, and attractive and, well, just nice. When we hear negative comments from our moms and daughters, it can take us to that place of insecurity, misery, and pain. When negative comments come at us, we can react with rage, fall into the pit of hurt feelings, resentment and despair. Or we can understand the context and take the sting out of the comment.

EXAMPLES OF PIVOTING

Our friend Angela is a loving daughter who cares deeply for her mom. Angela is an attractive and competent nurse who is highly respected at work. Recently, she heard from a friend that her mom, who is going through a difficult time, is now telling everyone that Angela is difficult, and will never be able to keep a man and get married. Ouch. Angela could take these comments to heart and be furious, but she knows how to edit and pivot where her mom's pronouncements are concerned. The context here is that mom has been divorced and on her own for years; she's the one who now feels like an old maid. Angela has no interest in getting married and turns annoyance into compassion. Can you do this when your mom or daughter insults you?

Lindsey and Leslie are both super sensitive about making mistakes, being in the wrong. Where does this hypersensitivity come from? It doesn't matter. It's part of us. For a mother/daughter duo who used to hurt each other regularly and dwell on each outrage for weeks, we now have to constantly remind ourselves that to err is human. We put our instant reactions into context. It's not what someone else is making us feel, it's how we manage what we hear.

From 1-10 Rank You and Your Mom's EQ In These Areas

TYPE	DESCRIPTION	MOM	DAUGHTER
Outlook	How positive and supportive are you		
Social Intuition	How aware are you of others' feelings		
Self-awareness	Do you know how to describe your feelings & behave appropriately		
Sensitivity to context	Can you tell what's really going on		
Self-control	How well do you manage impulses		
Moods	How moody are you		

LEARNING ACTIVITIES

KEEP "MY STORY" GOING

Now, add this information about styles to your ongoing "My Story." Include the mother's personality and parenting style as well as daughter's. Reflect on what you have learned and make a chart on how you are alike and how you are different. Give that some thought. What are your points of agreement and disagreement? Are they major or minor? Are these areas of disagreement causing relationship chasms? Why? How is your story progressing? What new insights have you gained about the mother-daughter relationship? What new information are you finding that is useful as you work through your relationship? Is your thinking changing? Why or why not?

Emotional & Personality Styles

JOURNAL PROMPTS: EQ

1. Do you consider yourself to be in control of your emotions? What about your mom?
2. Are you self-aware? Can you admit your faults?
3. Are you resilient? Is your mom or her mom resilient? Explain.
4. How is your outlook on life? How is your mom's outlook?
5. How do people react to you? How do they react to your mom?
6. When you're in an argument with your mom or daughter can you adapt to new information and calm down?

ADD TO YOUR DICTIONARY

Hypervigilant
Empath
Dismissive
Disparaging
Self-awareness
Social awareness
Hypersensitivity
Catastrophizer

FOUR COMPONENTS OF EMOTIONAL INTELLIGENCE (EQ)		
	PERSONAL COMPETENCE	SOCIAL COMPETENCE
RECOGNITION	**SELF-AWARENESS** The ability to recognize and understand your moods, emotions and drives. as well as their effects on your behavior and others. • Self-confidence • Emotional self-awareness • Accurate self awareness	**SOCIAL-AWARENESS** The ability to understand the feelings, needs, and emotional makeup of others, skill in empathy. • Empathy • Service orientation • Organizational awareness
REGULATION	**SELF-MANAGEMENT** The ability to control or redirect disruptive impulses, and moods, and the ability to think before acting/reacting. • Self-control • Trustworthiness • Conscientiousness • Adaptability • Initiative • Drive and motivation • Growth mindset	**RELATIONSHIP MANAGEMENT** Proficiency in managing and building relationships to produce desired results in others. Ability to communicate effectively • Influence • Inspirational leadership • Building bonds • Team work and collaboration • Mentoring • Conflict management

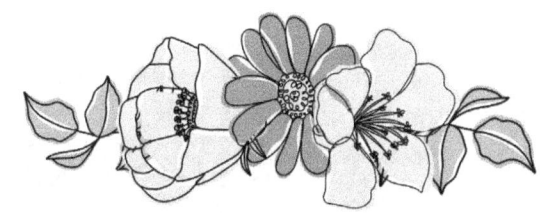

CHAPTER 8
COMMUNICATION

Reading Assignment: Chapter 4 of *The Mother Daughter Relationship Makeover* page 57

COMMUNICATION

Communication influences everything, from the very moment that you are born. The way people communicate with you and the way you communicate with others determine how you're going to get along with them, make them feel, and how they will end up treating you. Communication will affect your career, your role in your family, and your romantic relationships. We first learn to communicate from our parents and caregivers, then the people around us as we grow. If people around you are positive, healthy communicators, life will be pleasant. If they are not positive communicators, a host of issues can arise.

HOW MANY WAYS DO WE COMMUNICATE

Before we get into what we say and what people hear, let's consider nonverbal communications like body language and behavior. Here are some examples. Physically, are you/your daughter open to hugging, smiling, laughing and cuddling? We don't mean just with animals. Are you openly welcoming with your facial expressions and physical body language to your children, grandchildren and co-workers? The expression on your face communicates your feelings; and make no mistake, we all know when someone is irritated, doesn't want to listen, is dismissive or brushes you off. Moms can shut you down with just a look, and that behavior begins very early in daughters' lives. Daughters, too, especially teens, communicate through abrupt angry gestures that can make moms feel just awful all the time. Consider these forms of communication.

- Gestures
- Facial expressions
- Text messages
- Voice mail
- Physical pushing away
- Slamming doors

LASTING IMPACT OF NEGATIVE COMMUNICATION

Children who experience dismissive non-verbal communication often have low self-esteem. They may feel undervalued, unheard, or misunderstood. They may grow up secretly angry at everyone. If your needs and feelings were ignored in childhood, you may repeat this pattern in romantic relations and sometimes at work as well.

How many chronically angry people do you know who communicate with negative non-verbal body language and behaviors? Imagine being resentful toward loving people who have done you no harm? Imagine living the same hurtful relationship dynamic over and over. And it's not only children who feel dismissed. Adults who regularly receive spiteful, hurtful or blaming voicemails, emails, or texts from loved ones can also question their own value or harbor angry feelings of being wronged and project this hurt out into the world.

FOUR COMMON COMMUNICATION STYLES

1. Assertive: The assertive communicator stands up for their needs and rights while maintaining respect for others. Communication is thoughtful without any hurtful comments. This style is positively correlated with people who feel their opinions are heard, that everyone in the conversation matters, and that everyone is valued.

2. Loving: A style that clearly sends the message, 'You are important to me. I care what you think and feel.' Loving communication does not mean you do not have difficult conversations. It means you have them with care and respect.

3. Aggressive: An aggressive communicator stands up for their beliefs, needs, or perceived rights, but without knowing it may be violating the rights of others. An aggressive communicator is often filled with anger, disrespect, and causes fear in others.

4. Passive: In this style the communicator puts the rights of others before their own, minimizing their own needs. A passive communicator has lower self-esteem, feels disrespected, and does not learn to voice their needs. One may be passive for many reasons including the need for safety.

From 1-10 Rank Your Mom's And Your Communication Style

TYPE	DESCRIPTION	MOM	DAUGHTER
Assertive	Communication is thoughtful without hurtful comments.		
Loving	Loving communication means you handle them with care and respect.		
Aggressive	An aggressive communicator is often filled with anger, disrespect, & causes fear in others.		
Passive	A passive communicator has lower self-esteem, feels disrespected, and does not learn to voice their needs.		

YOUR BOOK REVIEW

When you read Chapter 4, did you think about how well, or badly, communication is going in your mother-daughter relationship? How did you get to this place? What memories do you both have about early communication? Communication includes so much more than verbal exchanges. Body language, facial expressions, and tone of voice convey strong messages.

Once again, we're sharing our own communication struggles as an example for you to understand how miscommunication can happen. Here we explain more about communication styles for you to consider. Make notes about the styles that apply to you in your mother-daughter relationship.

MORE COMMUNICATION STYLES TO CONSIDER

1. Combative: I am quick to react to any perceived slight. I'll defend any position I have, and I hate to think I am ever in the wrong. Aggressive communication involves expressing thoughts and needs in a forceful and confrontational manner, often disregarding the feelings and opinions of others. This style can intimidate and alienate others, damaging relationships and hindering effective communication.

2. Conflict avoiding, non confrontational: I'll do anything to avoid a fight. I don't like to see people fighting and don't want to get involved or take sides. That makes me appear and act passive. Passive communication involves avoiding conflict, keeping opinions to oneself, and prioritizing others' needs over one's own. Moms/daughters with this style often struggle to express their thoughts or assert boundaries, leading to potential frustration and misunderstandings.

3. Controlling: I want things to go right, be done in the right way, my way. I may be something of a perfectionist or an extreme worrier about what can go wrong if I'm not in control. Narcissistic: Narcissism is more than just being self-centered or selfish. It means you can only think about yourself in every equation in a toxic way. There is no one else to consider. You don't really care about other people's feelings. Narcissists lie about you to your friends and loved ones to cause trouble and make themselves look good.

4. Passive-aggressive: I seem sweet, but underneath my nice exterior, I can be as sharp as a serpent's tooth. I'm the person who purchases donuts for you and then gives your share to someone else. I will open a door for you and then close it on your foot. I confuse people with my niceness. Passive-aggressive communication combines elements of both passive and aggressive styles. It involves indirect expressions of negative feelings, sarcasm, and subtle undermining behaviors. This style can create confusion and erode trust within relationships.

5. Sensitive/oversensitive: I am sensitive and let everyone know it. I may use my sensitivity as a weapon against you, always claiming to be hurt by something you or someone else has done. I may also be sensitive to slights but not dare show it.

6. Victim: I feel like a victim. I do everything for everybody else and resent it. I both play the victim and feel the victim. People pleasers, codependents, and enablers often feel victimized by their over-helping.

7. Patient/impatient: I am patient and loving and willing to hear your side or let you find your way, or I am impatient and grab things out of your hands when you can't do something fast enough to suit me.

8. Empathic: I am empathic. People who are empathic can also be people pleasers. Being too empathic and people-pleasing can be problematic. If you feel your daughter's pain too much and want to shield her from disappointment, you may prevent her from learning to live with the setbacks and pain that is inevitable in every person's life.

9. Emotionally intelligent communication: Emotionally intelligent communication emphasizes understanding and empathizing with others' emotions. It involves active listening, observing non-verbal cues, and responding in a sensitive and supportive manner. Emotionally intelligent communicators create a safe and inclusive environment where all voices are heard and valued.

Assessing your mother-daughter communication style is essential for relationship growth. Here is more information to help you as you explore this topic.

HEALTHY COMMUNICATION 101

Consider Your Audience - what does that mean? It's crucial to communicate in a style that will get you the result you want. Understanding your audience has to do with using a style that will appeal and make the listener feel understood and safe.

For example, if you know your mom or daughter has an aggressive style of communication, then it's important to set times to talk about important issues and prepare her for the conversation. Don't put her in a position where she will feel defensive and immediately try to take control of the conversation. Prepare her for the talk, the subject, even set ground rules so a simple talk doesn't escalate into a fight.

Active Listening - Active listening is a communication skill that involves being fully engaged when someone else is speaking, with the intent to understand what they are saying and why. It's more than just hearing the words; it's about actively processing and seeking to understand the meaning and intent behind them. It makes people feel heard and understood and leads to stronger relationships.

A good example is to listen and then repeat back what you think they said or are trying to get across before answering. Active listening means you've set aside the impulse to interrupt, debate, and refute. You're just listening even if you think the other person is wrong.

USE EMOTIONAL INTELLIGENCE

How do you use emotional intelligence for effective communication? As well as understanding your audience, you want to limit your exchanges to a level equal to the other person's ability to respond. You don't ask more of someone than they can handle.

For example, if you know your daughter has a limited capacity for stress or criticism, take that into account before confronting her. Remember what you want to achieve and rephrase your requests to the highest level of positivity. "I would love it if you would…"

What is the hardest communication style to deal with? Aggressive. It's easy to spot an aggressive communicator, as you will usually feel anxious at the prospect of dealing with them. Aggressive communicators have no problem calling you out, being loud, holding prolonged eye contact, and other slightly menacing behaviors. Do you know any aggressive communicators?

What is the most effective communication style? Assertive Communication Style. The assertive communication style is widely considered to be the most effective. This style is direct and straightforward without being domineering. Assertive communicators know how to get what they want, but not at the expense of others on their team. Do you know any effective communicators?

What is an unhealthy communication style? Known as 'The Four Horsemen', these are criticism, contempt, defensiveness and stonewalling. If consistently experienced, these counterproductive behaviors can have a very negative impact on a relationship. Do you know anyone who does these?

What is the healthiest style of communication? Assertive Communication. Assertive communication is born of high self-esteem. It is the healthiest and most effective style of communication - the sweet spot between being too aggressive and too passive. When we are assertive, we have the confidence to communicate without resorting to games or manipulation. Do you think you have assertive communication? If not, why not?

Here are some tips for improving communication between mothers and daughters:

Be aware of body language: Children can communicate their needs and feelings through body language, facial expressions, and gestures. They also can read adult body language well. Be aware of how you hold your body, use your hands, and react. Anger is easy for children to spot. So is disappointment. Think about what you convey.

Be appreciative: Show appreciation for your mom's/daughter's accomplishments, no matter how small. Effort is essential for positive growth. We all fail. That is how we learn. Keep an open mindset and be encouraging.

Be present: Be there for your mom or daughter when she needs you.

Talk about everyday things: Find something to chat about regularly, even if it's brief and casual.

Discuss your communication styles: Talk about your communication styles when you're not upset.

Create a plan: Decide how you will handle issues that you don't agree on.

Take a break: If you're in conflict with your mother/daughter, take a break to discuss your plan.

Mood Meters: Start and end the day with emotional check-ins. Many grammar schools use these tools, and they are a great way to build a vocabulary of emotions which supports positive communication skills.

COMMUNICATION BOUNDARIES

Sadly, we know from experience that when communication habits go off the rails, yelling and screaming, name-calling, disparaging, blaming, shaming, and other toxic and hurtful behaviors become regular occurrences. This is not acceptable nor will you get what you want by acting this way. Here are our firm communication boundaries.

1. Be Clear About How You Expect To Be Treated
- If voices are raised, I will exit the conversation.
- I will not tolerate any disrespect or name-calling.
- Define any off-limit topics.

2. Define When and How You Communicate
- Set times to talk: I'm free in the evenings.
- Don't call when I'm at work or busy with kids.
- If you don't want to talk, use text or email.

3. Say What You Mean Without Being Mean
- Be honest but not hurtful. "I love you but don't have time for…

- I really don't like it when you…
- Please don't complain about your sister, brother, husband…

4. Clarify Consequences for Crossing Boundaries
If mom or daughter won't respect these communication boundaries create a consequence.
- If you yell at me, I will have to hang up.
- If you call me at work, I don't take the call.
- If you continue to complain about…I will need to take a break.
- If you hurt my feelings, I won't be able to do…

5. Stay Calm and Consistent
Always deliver your boundaries in a calm, assertive tone. If your mom/daughter tries to escalate, stick to your boundary without engaging in their disrespect. Lindsey and Leslie both use breaks to end disrespectful conversations. And of course, they took a long break from each other when communication got too heated.

JOURNAL PROMPTS: COMMUNICATION

1. Describe your family's communication style. Judgmental, supportive, accepting, combative, teasing are just a few possibilities. Where does it come from? Dad or mom? How do family members get along at the dinner table? How do you feel when you're together?

2. How does your mom/daughter communicate with you? Impatient, patient, supportive, nagging, yelling are a few possibilities. Give some examples of how she sounds.

3. What would you like communication with your mom/daughter to sound like? Give some examples.

4. What do you hear when your mom/daughter talks to you now?

5. Write a letter to your mom/daughter about how her communications make you feel. But don't send it. This is for you.

6. What are some words your mom said that you will never forget? You can write a little story here. And you can tell a positive one, like the day you became a blabbermouth for life. Also add how this made you feel.

Use as many specific examples as you can to support your thoughts. Early messages often last a lifetime. We need to understand why we are having the feelings we are in our relationship. Examining communication styles and miscommunications can reveal much that can lead to healing.

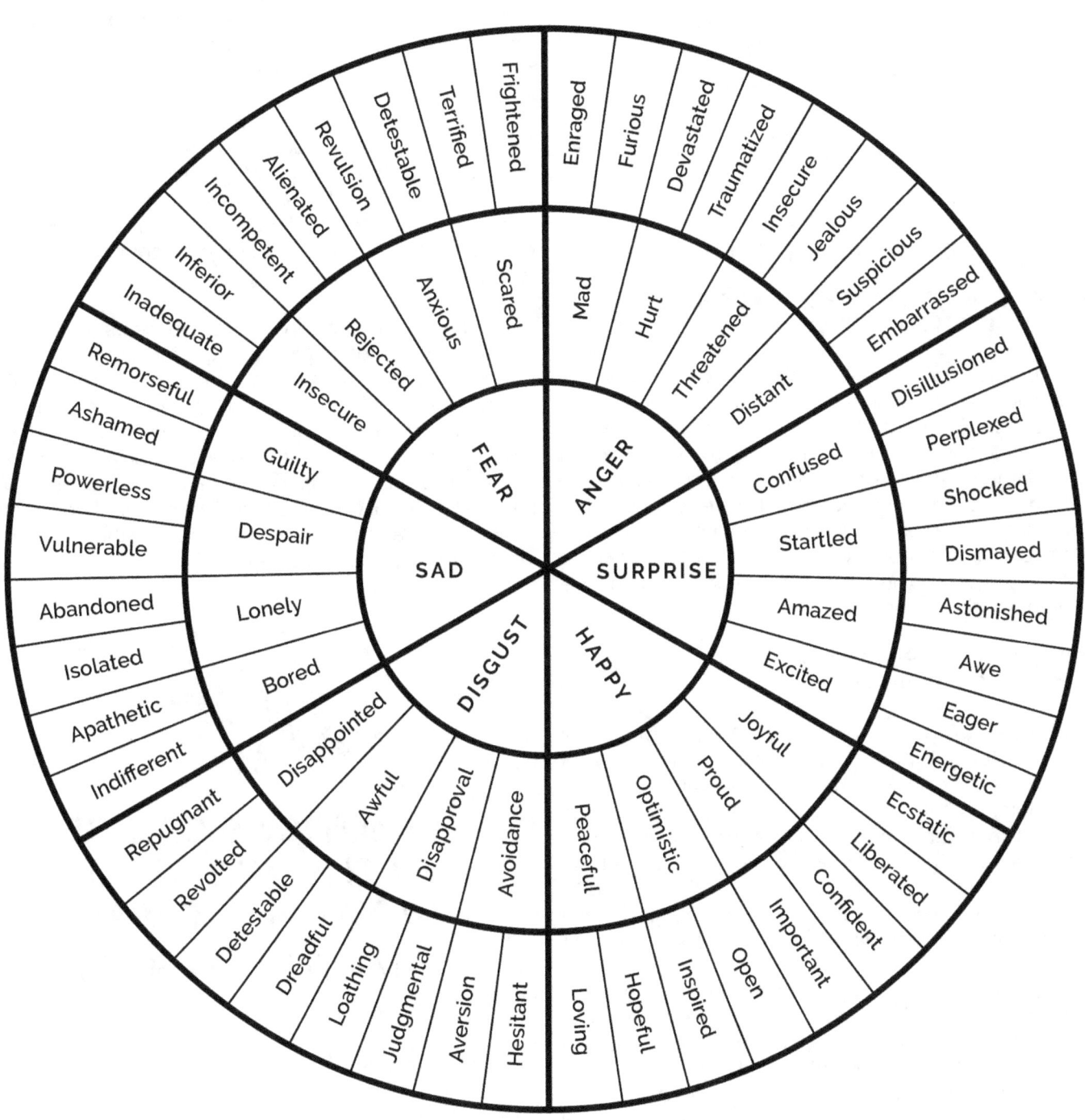

LEARNING ACTIVITIES

IDENTIFYING THE MOTHER-DAUGHTER COMMUNICATION STYLES

Carry on writing your story and include a page on how your communication with your mother or daughter has changed over the years. What was your communication like when you were little, a teenager, a 20-something, adult? Consider if your communication has become more aggressive, more insulting, critical, manipulative, or anything else you feel has been a destructive communication development or pattern. If it's become more positive, please note that as well! Do this from whatever point of view you need help with–as a daughter, mother, or grandmother.

HOW MOOD AFFECTS YOUR COMMUNICATION STYLE

Mood Meters – You saw one above. A mood meter is a great tool for getting a better understanding of your emotions. Being self-aware means that you are better able to understand what you are feeling and why. This leads to clear communication about your needs. Just search for Mood Meters on the Internet and you will find lots of tools to use. Or even better, create your own Mood Meter adding new emotion words as you increase your understanding of emotions. You can begin with the Mood Wheel on page 43.

Begin by keeping a daily mood meter log for one week. Check in with yourself before you leave for the day. Be sure to note why you are feeling that emotion. Then at the end of the day do another check-in. What has happened to cause the emotions that you are identifying? Write a personal 'Glow and Grow' reflection. What happened that made you feel good (glow)? What happened that changed this feeling? How can you better manage your emotions (grow)? Be sure to acknowledge what day it is, how you feel on Monday versus Friday, a weekend versus a busy work day, etc.

IDENTIFYING OUR MOOD HABITS

How many moods do humans have and why is it important to measure emotional regulation? Psychiatric science points to four core emotions: happiness, sadness, fear, and anger, which are differentially associated with three core effects: reward (happiness), punishment (sadness), and stress (fear and anger). However, the words we use in identifying our emotions matter. When we are feeling good there are so many words beyond happy. Positive emotions may come from being invited to an event, getting good news from a doctor, passing a test, getting that new job, enjoying time with a special person and more. Are you really feeling joy, calmness, contentment, gratitude, tranquility, or relief in your life?

Expanding your vocabulary of emotions helps you to better identify what emotion you are experiencing with greater precision, which leads to better understanding. Having gratitude is very different from being relieved – which both are positive feelings. Depending upon whose research you study, there are many categorical lists. Scientific reports state that we as humans can potentially experience and name a total of 34,000 emotions. The mood wheel graphic opposte illustrates emotions and the feeling they stem from, which do you experience the most?

"EMOTIONS CAN GET IN THE WAY OR GET YOU ON THE WAY."
-MAVIS MAZHURA

MY WEEK OF EMOTIONS				
Using the zones of regulation fill out the calendar to document the zones you go through in a week. The goal is to try and stay in or get back to the second zone.				
ZONES OF REGULATION	Low energy & motivation to participate	Attentive & feeling positive overall	Uncomfortable & needs to focus	Full of negative emotions & may react harshly
SUNDAY Today I felt _____ _____ _____ To stay in the second zone I tried to: _____ _____ _____ _____	**MONDAY** Today I felt _____ _____ _____ To stay in the second zone I tried to: _____ _____ _____ _____	**TUESDAY** Today I felt _____ _____ _____ To stay in the second zone I tried to: _____ _____ _____ _____	**WEDNESDAY** Today I felt _____ _____ _____ To stay in the second zone I tried to: _____ _____ _____ _____	**THURSDAY** Today I felt _____ _____ _____ To stay in the second zone I tried to: _____ _____ _____ _____
FRIDAY Today I felt _____ _____ _____ To stay in the second zone I tried to: _____ _____ _____ _____	**SATURDAY** Today I felt _____ _____ _____ To stay in the second zone I tried to: _____ _____ _____ _____	**THOUGHTS ON THIS WEEK** This week I felt I did well at : _____ _____ _____ _____ Next week I want to work on : _____ _____ _____ _____		

CHAPTER 9
GETTING HONEST ABOUT THE SECRETS AND LIES

Reading Assignment: Chapter 5 of *The Mother Daughter Daughter Relationship Makeover* page 75

In Chapter 5, we share our family and personal lies and secrets. Why? Because lies and secrets can undermine the mother-daughter relationship and can be used for all the wrong reasons. In our story, Leslie didn't investigate her daughter's life as Lindsey was experimenting with drugs and becoming increasingly unstable. Why? Read her story and you will better understand. Take some notes as you read.

HONESTY CREATES TRUST AND SAFETY

Honesty is a vital component of communication. You may not have thought about this before. If we're not telling the truth, we can't help and protect each other. This is the case with every aspect of life from work to politics to global events. Honesty empowers us. We can fix and find solutions for problems only when we have all the facts. As we have indicated in the previous chapter, communication is more than what we say. It's also how we act, including our facial expressions, grunts, sighs, body language, reactions. Your mom or daughter's reactions reveal a great deal about how they feel and what they want to happen through many forms of communication. Approval or disapproval can be shown in just the pursuing of lips or angry huff, as well as a laugh, a hug, a cheer. And each kind of communication affects our mood and self-esteem.

HIDDEN FACTS AND FEELINGS CREATE DISTRUST

We also communicate our lack of trust in each other by the things we don't say. When we don't share what's really going on, we put ourselves and our loved ones in danger. Making connections helps us be healthy, loved, and safe. If a son or daughter is drinking and taking a sibling for a joyride and no one tells the truth, tragedy can result. Many teens don't tell their parents when siblings drink or use drugs.

Teen or parental drinking affects family safety and may be something moms don't explore deeply enough with their daughters. Behavior and safety is another minefield for deception. The fact is we all lie. Teenage daughters lie to their mothers about what they're up to. Mothers lie to their daughters about what they are up to. Mothers also lie about the things their husbands and relatives do. Daughters lie about their feelings while acting them out in ways that baffle their moms. "I didn't know she felt that way," is a common mom reaction to learning those deeply held secrets that had tragic consequences.

Here's a fact. Every day of our lives we tell lies and keep secrets – some small and some larger. We tell lies for a variety of reasons. Tiny lies often keep the peace. Or keep us from hurting someone. Or keep us out of trouble. Secrets are often like lies. We tell them to gain control or power or revenge. Lies and secrets create drama in our lives. They can make us feel important or left out.

Secrets and lies can also be used out of a misguided intention of protection. It's natural to want to keep upsetting information from someone you love. However, without all the information, a mother or daughter can find herself without the vital facts she needs. For example, withholding information about mental health or addiction in the family, can be confusing for a daughter who finds herself struggling with one of these things and not knowing why or how it happened. Moms who don't share information about predators in the family put their daughters at risk. Saying an angry drunk is just "tired" prevents children from understanding what's happening and finding their own solutions.

What lies and secrets do you have? How do you justify to yourself that it was ok to have them? What were some of the consequences of telling them?

JOURNAL PROMPTS: SECRETS AND LIES

1. What secrets has your mother told you never to tell anyone else? Why did she tell you? How did they affect you then and how are they affecting you now?

2. Do you think your mother is keeping other secrets? Have you asked her?

3. What secrets about abuse or discrimination, bullying, or mental health and addiction are hidden in your family tree of mental health?

4. How many secrets are you keeping? What lies do you tell? Why?

5. How many secrets and lies do you suspect your daughter may be keeping? What are they? Has she experienced rape or abuse, and would she feel she can tell you?

6. What would happen if you came clean to your mother/daughter about your secrets and lies? What would be the best thing? What would be the worst thing?

LEARNING ACTIVITIES

REFLECTIVE SENTENCE STARTERS

Lies and Secrets Prompts

1. The biggest lie I ever told my mom was:

2. The biggest lie my mom ever told me was:

3. Three secrets I am keeping from everyone are:

4. A secret I wish I didn't know is:

5. How do I know that a secret is true?

6. A lie that really hurt me was :

7. A lie I told to hurt someone was :

GENERAL PROMPTS TO GET YOU THINKING

If you open your journal and feel stuck, try using one of these sentence starters.

1. Today I am inspired by:

2. There is no easy way to say this:

3. How do I know:

4. I thought it would be fun to share:

5. I often ask myself:

6. I am curious about:

7. I wonder why:

8. There is one thing that annoys me:

9. When I need inspiration I:

10. For me change is :
11. When I was younger:
12. When I am older:
13. How often have I heard:
14. It's silly to think:
15. One of the earliest lessons I have learned:
16. Why have I never considered:
17. An interesting thing that happened to me:
18. I laugh when I hear:
19. That always makes me cry:
20. What can I do differently next time:

CONTINUE "MY STORY"

Add to your ongoing "My Story." Add what you have learned about lies and secrets. How have family and personal lies and secrets impacted you and your mother-daughter relationship? What is your plan for dealing with this?

LITTLE SECRETS GROW UP TO BE BIG LIES

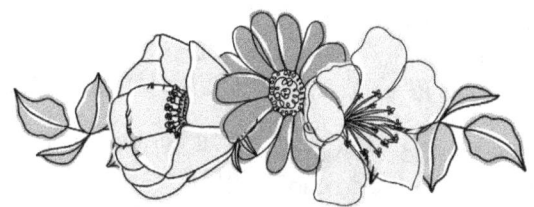

CHAPTER 10
STEP 2: AREAS OF CONFLICT: FOOD & WEIGHT

Reading Assignment: Chapter 6 of *The Mother Daughter Relationship Makeover* page 93

YOUR FAMILY'S EATING HABITS

What are the eating habits in your family? Does your mom eat more than she needs and feeds you more than you need? You are likely to follow her lead. Does she have a problem with self-regulation, a restrictor who worries that you're too big? Is food an expression of love for her? Is acquiring food a joy or constant source of anxiety for her? All of these situations and many more will determine whether food and weight are an issue in your relationship.

The way food was treated in the history of your family also determines how you're going to feel about it. For many cultures, food is love. Cooking is a daily family affair and all aspects of the meal from the shopping to the preparing, serving, eating are part of an important ritual that keeps the family united. If your family had plenty of money for food, a great love of food and cooking, but also a respect for moderation, you may have positive feelings about food. If there wasn't enough money, food was scarce, or parents who didn't care about it, you may have complicated feelings about it. In short, all of the ways we are raised around food and nutrition impacts us and has potential for mother/daughter conflict.

Families where eating is proof of love and everyone is big can be challenging for daughters who don't have a big appetite, or want to regulate their weight. We tend to look like the people around us.

WEIGHT

How you eat and manage food also controls your weight. Do you come from a family of runners and health nuts who count their calories and wouldn't touch a carb to save their lives? Or, are you from a long line of overeaters? We don't use that word in a judgemental way. Seventy-five percent of Americans fit into a category defined as obese. That means you are likely to have some members in your family who indulge with food, could lose some weight but do not allow dietary changes or discussion around the issue. Weight can be an issue for any family.

In addition, many moms use weight as a way to control their daughters; and we'll get more into this below. The fact remains that food plays a vital role in our lives and in our relationship with our mom/daughter. In our case, while we have had our conflicts over diet and nutrition in the past, we are proud that we have been able to develop a healthy relationship with food and with each other. We have the ability to support each other when we are watching our weight, and we agree that indulging on occasion is both satisfying and fun.

CONTROL

Food is one of the primary ways moms and daughters can control each other. Food is a way to create emotional connection or punishment. Feeling bad? Let me get you some comfort food. Didn't pass your test, no dessert for you. Food can easily be a reward, a bribe, or a way to shame someone terribly. You can manipulate or guilt trip with food.

Ever heard mom say, "But I spent all day on this..." Or mom spent all day on something and daughter eats it in five seconds while scrolling on her phone, then leaves abruptly, without saying thank you. Leslie knows how this feels. Resentment can build. And we have to add the restrictors and how annoying they can be, whether it's mom or daughter. Restricting your own, or other people's food can be unhealthy when you overdo it, and can lead to serious health problems, and of course, conflict. We know because we've been there on this one.

As you can see, food is deeply personal, and we all have experiences with family and food that have brought great pleasure and extreme anxiety. You don't have to have a food disorder to have a complicated relationship with food. Regulating what we eat is a challenge for all of us. Having a great relationship with your body image is rare, so we must add a note on how our ambition to be beautiful according to trending values can bring on food disorders. Now is the time to find some awareness around your habits and culture and see how they affect your mother-daughter relationship. Take the assessment below by briefly describing how each area affected you and your mom's/daughter's relationship with food and each other.

Generational Assessment

AREA	FOOD
Cultural Influences	
Economic Influence	
Mom/ Daughter Control	
Family Food Habits?	
Overeaters Undereaters	

WHEN FOOD ISSUES DRIVE YOU APART

Food and weight issues with your mom/daughter can feel both frustrating and overwhelming. Being pushed to eat, or nagged about being too heavy by a mom or daughter can drive a wedge between you that makes you want to avoid talking or getting together. We will explore triggers, conflict resolution, and boundaries in the coming chapters. For now, think about this:

IF YOU'RE EATING HEALTHY AND YOUR FAMILY ISN'T

Complaining won't help. Get your own food. Bring it with you if you're visiting. Offer substitutions at family meals to tempt loved ones to try something new and healthier. You don't have to give in to control or peer pressure. Changing habits takes time.

IF YOUR FAMILY IS DRINKING AND YOU'RE SOBER

Lindsey and Leslie remember being invited to a party in our honor which turned out to be a wine tasting after we specifically told the host we don't drink. It was a party, but not for us. If your family members are drinkers, you don't have to spend too much time with them. You can stop in and not stay. You can leave early. Of course, you can bring your own drinks. In our family we all stopped drinking to support the sober members. You can make choices here when loved ones make you feel bad. This goes for both moms and daughters.

IF PEER PRESSURE BRINGS YOU DOWN

After being told she had "thunder thighs," Leslie starved herself for two years. Who was she hurting, only herself. So what are some solutions to food conflicts? If you want a good relationship? Stop nagging, commenting, offering food, withholding it, or judging other people's eating habits or appearance. We're all the bosses of our own bodies. Live and let live.

6 THINGS YOU SHOULD NEVER SAY TO YOUR MOM OR DAUGHTER ABOUT EATING

1. **You're eating too much.** This is choice and portion shaming.

2. **That will make you fat.** This fuels anxiety and encourages food disorders.

3. **You're going to regret eating that later.** Turns meals or snacking into opportunities for anxiety and conflict.

4. **A moment on the lips... (A lifetime on the hips)** This is an old-fashioned homily that is fear fearmongering.

5. **Why can't you eat more like...** Comparisons between you and others are especially galling.

6. **You are too skinny/fat you should eat more/less.** Not helpful. This is both controlling and insecurity making.

6 THINGS YOU SHOULD SAY TO YOUR MOM OR DAUGHTER ABOUT EATING

1. **That dish looks great, can I try it?** Shows interest around food not judgment.

2. **I really appreciate you cooking/buying this.** This praises effort instead of judging choices.

3. **I admire how you always make meals feel special.** This connects food to love and family.

4. **I understand eating can be stressful for you, let me know how I can help.** This acknowledges her struggle with eating instead of shaming it.

5. **I love sharing food and meals with you.** Reinforces how meals can be bonding time.

6. **You're so good at listening to your body.** Reinforces intuitive eating and trusting yourself

Your assessment above may enlighten you to what's going on and help you find compassion and understanding

JOURNAL PROMPTS : WEIGHT AND FOOD

1. How did your mom and grandma feel about their weight and food?

2. Did food play a big part in your family/relationship with mom?

3. How is your relationship with food?

4. Does food ever make you unhappy and you secretly think your eating is disordered in some way? Explain how eating makes you feel now.

5. Does your mother/daughter support your eating habits? Explain how.

6. Is this an area where you would like to make changes? What kind of changes would you make?

UPDATING "MY STORY"

Time to add this new information to your mother-daughter story. Start this section of your story off with a heading titled something like 'What I Didn't Know or didn't think about food and weight."

"TO EAT IS A NECESSITY BUT TO EAT INTELLIGENTLY IS AN ART"
-FRANÇOIS DE LA ROCHEFOUCAULD

CHAPTER 11
FINANCES & MONEY

Reading assignment: Chapter 7 of *The Mother Daughter Relationship Makeover* page 107

How much do you know about your family's history with money? Let's start thinking about it. Is money regulation one of the problems in your mother/daughter relationship? Money and lack of trust around it was the breaking point for Leslie and Lindsey. When mom holds the purse strings and daughter is unhappy about the allocation of funds, conflict can become war. We will talk about boundaries in a future chapter, but this is the time to think about your money habits and beliefs especially if this is an area of conflict for you.

MOTHER-DAUGHTER MONEY CONFLICTS

If mom is holding the purse strings in your family, she has control of who gets what. In the past it was usually the man of the family who had the power of the purse. The father, the grandfather (or grandmother if she inherited). These days it can be mom or dad. Some 40% of American moms are the sole breadwinners of their families. Obviously, when you are little, your mom manages the money; but as the years go by if there is no education around family finances, control issues are bound to arise.

A mom who continues to pay the bills for an adult daughter may feel entitled to have a say in her daughter's life choices. The same goes for daughters paying expenses for their moms. Gender and generational beliefs about money still pervade in many areas where the man of the family controls the finances for both mom and daughter. What is the case in your family?

Values and spending habits definitely have an impact on the mother/daughter relationship. Are you like your mom, or different? If she's one of the 40% who supports the family, is she fiscally responsible? Is she a reckless overspender? Does she favor a sibling over you in her spending? You may be very careful with money, like her, or you may love nothing more than to hit the mall with her for hours, either shopping for bargains or going overboard. We've seen both moms supported by successful daughters, and daughters living off moms who may or may not be happy about it.

GETTING INDEPENDENT

For us, becoming independent of each other, setting budgets, spending priorities and limits helped us establish guidelines for finances. Everyone should do this. We also set rules about who owns and gets what. Where our resources are shared, earned together, or planned for in the future, communication is key. We are mindful of each other's needs and sensitive about how much we can spend on ourselves and others. We talk about it, and plan around it.

Are you comfortable with the arrangement in your mother/daughter relationship? Remember honesty and communication are the keys to a healthy relationship. Be clear when it comes to money matters. The goal here is to get comfortable talking about money and practicing fiscal responsibility. We know how tough money talks can be, but they are so vital for a satisfying relationship. Empower your mother or daughter to feel comfortable talking to you about money.

HOW MONEY CAN BE TOXIC

Because money is so often tied to security and control, it can get toxic real quick. Here is a list of ways we think money gets toxic between mothers and daughters.

1. Control & Power Struggles
- Financial Dependence as Leverage: If a mother supports her granddaughter she may demand a say in the child's life, education, etc.

- Strings-Attached Giving: Gifts or money may come with unspoken obligations, like spending more time with the mother or following her advice.

- Withholding Money as Punishment: A mother might refuse financial help or cut off support as a way to manipulate behavior.

2. Guilt & Obligation
- Sacrifice as a Weapon: "I worked so hard to give you a better life, and this is how you repay me?" This can make daughters feel trapped between gratitude and resentment.

- Expecting Financial Payback: Some mothers believe daughters "owe" them financial support later, even if it was never discussed.

- Comparisons to Others: "Your cousin helps her mother more; why can't you?" This creates unnecessary guilt and competition.

3. Enmeshment & Lack of Boundaries
- Oversharing & Over-Involvement: Some mothers share too much about their own financial struggles, making daughters feel responsible for fixing them.

- No Financial Independence: A mother may discourage her daughter from making her own financial decisions, keeping her dependent.

- Treating Daughters Like a Retirement Plan: Some mothers expect daughters to take care of them financially, even if it harms the daughter's own stability.

4. Financial Inequality & Jealousy
- Resentment Over Success: If a daughter becomes more financially successful than her mother, it can create jealousy or insecurity. The mother might downplay her achievements or subtly sabotage her confidence.

- Criticism of Spending Habits: A mother may judge how her daughter spends money, especially if they have different views on saving, debt, or luxury purchases.

- Entitlement to Daughter's Money: A mother may expect financial support even if she doesn't need it, making the daughter feel guilty for setting boundaries.

5. Toxic Inheritance & End-of-Life Money Issues
- Unequal Distribution: If a mother favors one child financially, it can create lifelong tension between siblings.

- Avoidance of Hard Conversations: If money isn't discussed openly, surprises in inheritance, debt, or financial needs can lead to fights and broken relationships.

Take the assessment below by briefly describing how each area affected you and your mom's/daughter's relationship with money and finances.

Generational Assessment

AREA	MONEY
Cultural Influence on money habits	
Economic Influence Is money scarce?	
Mom/Daughter Control	
Family Money Habits?	
Has money become toxic in your family?	

5 IMPORTANT CONVERSATIONS TO HAVE ABOUT MONEY AND FINANCES

1. Basic understanding of personal finances. Research areas of personal finance. What does it mean to manage money?

2. How to make a budget. How much do we have to spend and what do we need to spend? Write it down.

3. How credit cards and credit work. You can get in trouble when you keep charging for items you can't afford. Learn about interest.

4. Understanding Overspending. Is shopping a dangerous entertainment? Explore shopping addiction.

5. Money Manipulation. Is someone guilt-tripping you over spending, or scrimping on spending? It's a hard conversation. Some moms/daughters spend with abandon and tell you everything they're doing for you. Others are cheapskates when they don't have to be.

JOURNAL PROMPTS: MONEY AND FINANCES

1. What did you learn about money from your mother?

2. Did your mom learn from her mother?

3. Do you have good financial skills? Does your mother/daughter?

4. Does dealing with money or talking about money make you uncomfortable? If so, why?

5. If you have great financial skills, how did you get them?

6. If you feel challenged by money or earnings, explain why. Bonus: Do you have financial skills you'd like to learn? If so, what are they?

CONTINUE "MY STORY"

Time to add this new information to your mother-daughter story. Start this section of your story off with a heading titled something like 'What I Didn't Know about our habits and relationship around finances and money.

CHAPTER 12
APPEARANCE & STYLE

Reading Assignment: Chapter 8 of **The Mother Daughter Relationship Makeover** page 119

Appearance and style often become a source of conflict between mothers and daughters because how you look symbolizes deeper issues like identity, control, societal expectations, and generational differences. While it may seem like a simple disagreement over clothing, makeup, or body image, these conflicts often reflect broader struggles over autonomy, self-expression, and cultural norms.

This is another area where control can become a serious issue. A rebellious daughter may revel in embarrassing her mom with her wild, and even, inappropriate style. A "free-spirited" mom may cause her daughter endless shame by running around in outfits designed for someone half her age. Moms or daughters may approve of the each other's appearance or find them not aligning with what they think is culturally acceptable, attractive or appropriate for their age or status. When they don't agree, battles can rage.

JUDGING A DAUGHTER'S APPEARANCE

Many moms see their daughters as extensions of themselves, that is normal. It's also normal to fear that the world will judge you based on your daughter's appearance. If you are a conservative mom and your daughter dresses in a provocative manner, her sexiness can be both distressing and shaming. Moms may worry that their daughters' values don't match theirs, but also fear for their safety. And safety is a legitimate concern. The way girls dress can attract predators. That being the case, where should moms draw the line with their protective instincts?

We think there is also a lot of comparison and projection when it comes to the style and appearance of mothers and daughters. We've seen plenty of moms who can't help airing their jealousy of their daughters' youth and beauty. And some like to live vicariously through their daughters' adventures and encourage a flamboyant style. What's your mom/daughter like? Is she worried about what everyone thinks? Judgmental moms may criticize or shame their daughters' appearance because she's more concerned about how it reflects on her than whether her daughter is happy and expressing herself in a healthy way.

There are also issues around how the family views appearance. Do moms/daughters conform to societal and cultural expectations of beauty? Attractiveness, too, can be an area of conflict especially if a mom/family feels their daughter doesn't take responsibility for modesty, looking good, or being healthy.

WHEN MOM'S APPEARANCE IS AN ISSUE

Mom's appearance can cause anxiety and frustration for daughters, too, because it touches on deeper emotional, psychological, and societal pressures. Appearance is not just about looks—it's about identity, aging, comparison, and even fear of the future. Let's begin with that fear of the future. An aging mother may remind her daughter that the roles are shifting or create a fear of what's to come. A daughter may subconsciously see her mom aging and be worried about what will happen to her in the future. In the social pressures and beauty department, a mom who doesn't conform to societal norms may embarrass her daughter and a mom trying too-hard could embarrass her daughter. It's hard to get right, isn't it? And, no one's perfect.

DO YOU COMPARE AND DESPAIR

Comparison and self-esteem were issues in our family. Being the daughter of a beautiful and stylish mom made both Leslie and Lindsey feel they were living in their mom's shadow and could never compete. Comparing yourself to a beautiful mom who's prettier than you can be a terrible experience. Having a mom who's hyper-focused on her daughter's appearance is another recipe for body image and self-esteem issues.

Cultural and generational issues can also lead to conflict. Traditional moms who have rigid ideas about what looks are acceptable can frustrate their fashion forward daughters to no end. While moms who have plastic surgery or make other changes to their physical appearance may send mixed messages about self-acceptance or inspire their daughters to do the same. Basically, there is a lot going on under the surface about how we look on the outside.

6 THINGS TO REPHRASE OR NOT SAY TO YOUR MOM OR DAUGHTER ABOUT HER APPEARANCE

1. **You'd be so much prettier if...** This is what we call a backhanded compliment and it can be damaging to self-esteem.

2. **You look tired, old, or fat...** This is just stating flaws. It's not motivating; it's just wounding and reinforcing insecurities.

3. **You look like you've gained/lost weight.** This puts the focus on the body and not wellbeing.

4. **That hairstyle, makeup, or outfit doesn't suit you.** Again this is focusing on the negative and being judgemental.

5. **You're too old or young to wear that.** This is age shaming.

6. **Are you really going out in that?** It's policing. No one likes to be policed or judged.

6 THINGS YOU SHOULD SAY TO YOUR MOM OR DAUGHTER ABOUT HER APPEARANCE

1. **You look so happy. That's what I like to see.** Connects appearance to joy.

2. **Your smile lights up the room.** Commenting on a positive feature highlights your warmth.

3. **You have such a strong graceful presence.** Or any positive remark that affirms energy and personality. Things she can control.

4. **You look like yourself, and that's perfect.** It reassures that authenticity is enough.

5. **I love how you express yourself with your style.** This is affirming showing acceptance and approval.

6. **You radiate when you look healthy.** Focuses on wellbeing. Give this question of appearance and style some thought. What part has this played in your relationship? Are you comfortable with your your moms'/daughters' appearance and style? If not, why not? Let's explore in the assessment below. Briefly describe how each area affected you and your mom's/daughter's relationship with appearance and style.

Generational Assessment

AREA	APPEARANCE & STYLE
Has your culture influenced your style?	
Have your economics played a role in your style?	
Do you like your mom/daughter's appearance and style?	
Has your mom or daughter's appearance or style impacted you? How?	

"YOUR VOICE CAN LIVE ON IN THEIR HEAD, UNKNOWINGLY CHIPPING AWAY AT THEIR SELF-ESTEEM."

– SAMANTHA DECARO

JOURNAL PROMPTS : APPEARANCE

1. What did your mother teach you about appearance?

2. How comfortable are you with your looks?

3. Can you listen to your daughter's feelings about her appearance without being a fixer?

4. How can you help your daughter feel good about herself?

5. If you're a mother who is critical or a faultfinder, learning acceptance of others will help your daughter's self-esteem and acceptance of you.

6. Is there anything you'd like to do to improve your style? What's holding you back?

UPDATING "MY STORY"

Time to add this new information to your mother-daughter story. Start this section of your story off with a heading titled something like: What I Didn't Know about our habits and relationship around appearance and style.

CHAPTER 13
FRIENDS & ROMANTIC PARTNERS

Reading Assignment: Chapter 8 of *The Mother Daughter Relationship Makeover* page 119

Friends and romantic partners have incredible power over the way we feel and behave. A healthy, positive romantic partner and group of friends will support you and help you thrive, and your mom should be able to support them. An abusive or toxic friend or romantic partner can damage, even destroy precious relationships with family and your mom. You may come to blows over trying to save each other. Daughters-in-law can hijack your son. And boyfriends/husbands can drive a wedge between you and your mom/daughter. Think about your own relationships and who has your ear. Are they helpful or bring negative consequences to your mother/daughter relationship?

WHEN YOU FEEL BETRAYED

Have you had an experience where you thought someone was a great friend or partner, but who betrayed you? The didn't-see-that-coming phenomenon can be especially devastating. How many people do you know who had a moment with a friend where something happened that made them realize this person is not actually a good friend.

Maybe someone you cared about wasn't there for you when you needed them or worse, acted in a harmful or malicious way against you whether intentional or not. Maybe one day it becomes clear that you are the friend making all the effort and you're not even sure the friendship would continue if you stopped reaching out. In any case, here are some clear examples of what healthy and supportive friendships look like.

CHARACTERISTICS OF HEALTHY FRIENDSHIPS

- They are supportive of your needs and wishes.
- They listen and hear what you say.
- There is a healthy give-and-take.
- They bolster your self-esteem with positive feedback.
- They don't criticize you or your family.
- They are constant. They don't run hot and cold.
- Good friends don't ghost you or make you feel bad.
- Good friends don't bully you.
- They make you feel safe and good.

If your mom or daughter is constantly worried about the company you keep, she could be overly-anxious, but she could also see things that you don't. Instead of letting friends come between you and your mom or daughter, find ways to talk about them in healthy ways.

For example, it's OK to share with your mom or daughter, "Your friend "Jackie" engages in behavior that makes me worry for her safety and yours. How are you keeping safe when you are with her?" Or, "Mom, I know your friend "Kelly" drinks when you go out and I really don't want her driving you home. Would you be willing to take a cab when you're with her?"

WHAT MAKES A HEALTHY ROMANTIC RELATIONSHIP

A healthy romantic relationship is built on a foundation of mutual respect, trust, and effective communication. This sounds easy, but it's difficult for everyone to do all these things all the time. And, many people running around out there just looking for fun have little or no interest in respect, honesty, or effective communication. Think about what it means to see your beloved mom/daughter in a potentially dangerous relationship. Maybe you already know how painful it is to watch your mom or daughter struggle with the consequences of an unhealthy romantic relationship. Mom, of course, sets the example for how she wants and expects to be treated. If she has no boundaries and is treated badly or abused, her daughter may think abusive behavior is normal.

When a daughter is being mistreated, mom may be in a constant state of anxiety about the damage a destructive partner is causing. Basically being able to engage in a healthy romantic relationship is crucial for mom and daughter and for mom and daughter to have a peaceful relationship. Think about whether your friends cause conflicts and fear in your mother/daughter relationship. Let's consider what can be done to help. Here are some suggestions about how to address conflicts with this issue.

1. Communication
- Develop open and honest dialogue about feelings, needs, and expectations. This takes practice. Your mom/daughter needs to feel it's safe to share.
- Develop the skill of active listening—truly hearing and understanding your mom's/daughter's perspective.
- Address conflicts constructively rather than avoiding or escalating them.

2. Trust & Honesty
- Be reliable and keep your promises.
- Be transparent about your thoughts, feelings, and concerns.
- Give each other space to be independent while maintaining emotional security. This means don't nag. Don't be judgmental.

3. Respect & Support
- Value each other's opinions, even when they differ. This, too, takes practice.
- Encourage each other's personal growth and ambitions.
- Being kind and considerate, even in difficult moments.

4. Emotional & Physical Intimacy
- Share affection in ways that feel meaningful to your mom/daughter.
- Feel emotionally safe to be vulnerable. This is a gift you give each other.
- Mutual consent and comfort even when disagreeing.

5. Independence & Interdependence
- Maintain individuality and personal interests.
- Have a balance between togetherness and personal space.
- Support each other's friendships and external relationships.

6. Conflict Resolution Skills
- Address disagreements with patience and empathy.
- Focus on solutions rather than blame.
- Be willing to apologize and compromise when necessary.

7. Shared Values & Goals
- Align on core life values (e.g., family, career, lifestyle).
- Have mutual long-term aspirations and visions for the relationship.
- Navigate differences with respect and understanding.

8. Fun & Enjoyment
- Laugh together and create happy memories.
- Keep the relationship dynamic and exciting.
- Make time for quality moments despite busy schedules.

SIGNS OF PREDATORY & ABUSIVE BEHAVIOR

Recognizing the signs of toxic and predatory behavior is vital because knowing what to look out for helps protect your emotional, mental, and physical well-being. Being aware of these red flags allows you to set boundaries, make informed decisions, and avoid potentially harmful situations. As women, we have to protect our mental health and personal safety as well as that of our daughters. This means knowing how to communicate expectations of being treated with respect and dignity and how to avoid manipulation, control.

Friends & Romantic Partners

RED FLAGS OF PREDATORY & ABUSIVE BEHAVIOR

- Predators come on strong with charming behavior and love bombing.
- Predators are excellent liars.
- Predators create a false sense of intimacy they will use against you later.
- Predators have no boundaries and say and do whatever they want.
- Predators criticize your friends and/or family.
- Predators have control issues (control what you eat, wear, where you go).
- Predators control the finances.
- Predators aren't supportive of your needs and wishes.

This is a good time to think through your relationships and see who has the most influence on you and what that looks like. If this is a fighting issue for you and your mother/daughter, think about all the ways her opinion and influences differ from yours. What's going on? Awareness and understanding are the first steps to fixing both your heart and behavior.

Generational Assessment

AREA	FRIENDS
Has your culture influenced who you are friends with?	
Have economics played a part in your friends?	
Does your mom/daughter approve of your friends?	
Do you have toxic or supportive friends? Discuss	
Have your friends been a problem for your family?	

"A HEALTHY RELATIONSHIP WILL NEVER REQUIRE YOU TO SACRIFICE YOUR FRIENDS, YOUR DREAMS, OR YOUR DIGNITY."

– MANDY HALE

Generational Assessment

AREA	ROMANTIC PARTNERS
Do you date people like you? Same culture, religion?	
Do you date people with similar economic situations?	
Does your mom/daughter approve of your romantic partners?	
Do you have toxic or supportive romantic partners?	
Have your romantic partners been a problem for your family?	

JOURNAL PROMPTS: FRIENDS & ROMANTIC PARTNERS

1. Do you have friends that make you feel bad or cause trouble for you? Who are they?

2. Does your mother/daughter have friends that cause concern? Explain why.

3. Can you see any patterns with your mother's /daughter's friends and boyfriends/marriages and yours?

4. Are there any boyfriends/girlfriends (romantic relationships) that are unhealthy in the family? Describe them.

5. Have you ever talked to anyone about it if you have concerns?

6. If you fight with your mother/daughter, what is the biggest issue?

UPDATING "MY STORY"

Time to add this new information to your mother-daughter story. Start this section of your story off with a heading titled something like 'What I Didn't Know about our habits and conflicts around friends and lovers.

LEARNING ACTIVITIES

HEALTHY RELATIONSHIP BINGO

Use this activity on the next page to reflect on your relationships. Whether romantic, family, or friendships. Each square highlights what to look for, what to watch out for, and skills to strengthen. Circle what resonates with you, and notice patterns that show up.

```
ADD TO YOUR DICTIONARY
Toxic
Abusive
Controlling
Manipulative
Gaslight
Predator
```

HEALTHY RELATIONSHIP BINGO

WHAT TO LOOK FOR	RED FLAGS	RELATIONSHIP ROADBLOCKS	GREEN FLAGS	SKILLS TO STRENGTHEN
COMPATIBILITY	SELF-CENTERED OR NARCISSISTIC BEHAVIOR	GETTING DEFENSIVE	FEELING TRULY HEARD	PRACTICE APOLOGIZING WHEN YOU'RE WRONG
SHARED VALUES	CONSTANT JEALOUSY	AVOIDING OPEN COMMUNICATION	THOUGHTFUL & CONSIDERATE ACTIONS	SHARE YOUR FEELINGS OPENLY
ATTENTIVE LISTENING	BREAKING PROMISES	FREQUENT CONFLICTS	GENUINELY ENJOYING EACH OTHER'S COMPANY	SHOW RESPECT FOR ONE ANOTHER
MUTUAL TRUST	OVERLY CONTROLLING BEHAVIORS	LACK OF PERSONAL SPACE	ACCEPTANCE OF EACH OTHER'S INDIVIDUALITY	OFFER CONSISTENT SUPPORT
OPEN COMMUNICATION	TOO MUCH SCREEN TIME	BEING OVERLY CRITICAL	HONESTY AND COMMITMENT	LET GO OF THE NEED TO ALWAYS BE RIGHT

CHAPTER 14
DEPENDENCE & INDEPENDENCE

Reading Assignment: Chapter 10 of *The Mother Daughter Relationship Makeover* page 143

One of the hardest things for many moms to accept is that the daughter she created and carried so long is no longer hers. Take it from this mom, it's hard to internalize this basic fact. The minute your daughter is born, she is herself. You give her life and a name, but she develops on a path all her own. Emotionally, you may feel your daughter is always yours, but her sole job is to grow up, be independent, and function effectively with a life of her own. She may be like you, and she may be totally different, but in a healthy relationship, she outgrows your power over her. In fact, the older you both get the more your roles become reversed.

Mother/daughter roles shift over time and that, too, can create issues around responsibility and control. In addition, cultural and societal expectations may not match, causing daughters to feel guilty and disloyal for wanting independence when moms don't want their daughters to change or leave. Fear of change, communication challenges, and achieving individuality are all well within the normal experiences of mother/daughter dependence and independence. So, you see how tricky it can all get to stay emotionally connected while achieving the freedom to be yourself at any age.

EVERYONE IS CHANGING ALL THE TIME

Daughters experience profound changes as they mature, but the same thing goes for moms. While daughters are developing, moms are also experiencing countless personal life changes that motivate and influence their behavior. Physical changes and aging, illnesses, family relationships, spousal upheavals, divorce, economic ups and downs all impact the emotional development of moms. What did your mom go through, and how did it affect her behavior? Here's where you might consider not only how your mom's family and culture affected her parenting, but also what she was going through at various times of your life. Remember your mom was a parent for the first time when she had you and your siblings, but she may also have been working, been alone with responsibilities, and been terrified about so many things related to you, and also to her own journey. If you have a very controlling mom, know how challenging that is for daughters. We'll give you some signs of controlling moms in a minute. But first let's take a look at codependency and where that controlling begins.

UNDERSTANDING CODEPENDENCY AND ENABLING

Codependency is a relational pattern where one person becomes overly reliant on another for emotional validation, self-worth, or a sense of identity. This can happen in any relationship. Romantic and married partners can be overly clinging and dependent on each other and control each other. With regard to the mother-daughter relationship, either of you can be completely enmeshed with the other. Remember helicopter moms who hover over their children and can't let go. Moms can be involved with every aspect of their daughters' life from babyhood on. When moms don't change and let go as their daughters grow up, codependency becomes less about caring for and more about controlling.

SIGNS OF CONTROLLING MOMS

- Won't let her daughter question or discuss mom's decisions.
- Is demanding and insists on her daughter's obedience.
- Won't let her daughter make any of her own decisions.
- Won't allow her daughter to have her own choices about anything.
- Won't let her daughter have any independence at home or outside of home.
- Mom has to be right in all conversations and disputes.
- Dictates all aspects of her daughter's life.
- Helps without being asked.
- Has high standards and rigid rules that are impossible to live up to.
- Tells her daughter how to do things she already knows how to do.
- Doesn't respect her daughter's privacy.
- Doesn't allow critical thinking or her daughter's own opinions.
- Makes her daughter feel guilty and stupid.
- Manipulates by withdrawing love.
- Frequently uses the reason "Because I said so."
- Disparages and puts down.
- Uses punishment as coercion.
- Lacks empathy and behaves in uncaring ways.

HOW CODEPENDENCY DEVELOPS

- Codependency often stems from childhood dynamics, such as growing up in a home with emotional neglect, addiction, or enmeshment. It also can arise from a child's illness or special needs. Caretaking doesn't have to be seen as negative or toxic. Caretaking and closeness are healthy until they are taken to extremes.

- Codependent behaviors may be learned from parents or caregivers who modeled self-sacrifice or emotional caretaking. Doing too much, being too involved.

GIVER AND TAKER IN THE CODEPENDENT RELATIONSHIP

A codependent relationship often involves excessive emotional attachment in the form of caring. Your "caring" makes you involved with her every mood and need. She wakes up miserable for one reason or another, and you can't have a happy day until you can fix it. That means you will rearrange your day or make arrangements or spend money to "help" your loved one. If your mom or daughter has an addiction or mental illness your "caring" can ruin your life.

So, caretaking, people-pleasing, and difficulty setting boundaries are hallmarks of a codependent. One person (the "giver") may feel responsible for the emotions and well-being of the other (the "taker"), often at the expense of their own needs. Are you or your mom codependent? Think about this.

KEY SIGNS OF CODEPENDENCY:

1. Excessive Caretaking – Prioritizing others' needs while neglecting your own.

2. Difficulty Setting Boundaries – Struggling to say no, even when it harms you.

3. People-Pleasing Behavior – Seeking approval to feel worthy or valued.

4. Fear of Abandonment – Staying in unhealthy relationships due to fear of being alone.

5. Low Self-Esteem – Deriving self-worth from taking care of others.

6. Feeling Responsible for Others' Emotions – Believing it's your job to "fix" or "save" someone.

7. Control Issues – Trying to manage or control others' actions to feel secure.

8. Resentment & Burnout – Feeling drained or frustrated due to unbalanced giving.

IMPACT OF CODEPENDENCY

- Leads to one-sided, emotionally exhausting relationships.
- Prevents personal growth and healthy interdependence.
- Can create cycles of guilt, resentment, and emotional exhaustion.

Enabling is when someone unintentionally supports or allows another person's harmful or destructive behaviors to continue, often out of love, guilt, or fear of conflict. It's common in relationships where addiction, codependency, or unhealthy patterns exist. Again, this can arise from a child with perceived special needs or a mom's inability to set boundaries or guidelines or rules around harmful or destructive behaviors.

HOW ENABLING WORKS

Instead of helping a person grow or take responsibility for their actions, enabling shields them from consequences, which can keep them stuck in negative behaviors. I'll give an example of laziness: daughter won't do homework or walk the dog or do chores as a youngster, loudly complains and makes scenes. Mom picks up the slack to avoid getting yelled at and the habit develops that mom does and makes excuses for a daughter who doesn't want to be bothered. Don't get us wrong. This can happen with adult daughters who enable destructive habits in their moms.

EXAMPLES OF ENABLING BEHAVIOR:

1. Making Excuses – Covering for someone's bad behavior (e.g., calling in sick for a mom/daughter who is hungover).

2. Avoiding Conflict – Ignoring harmful actions just to keep the peace.

3. Taking Over Responsibilities – Handling tasks the other person should be doing (e.g., constantly bailing them out financially).

4. Minimizing the Problem – Downplaying destructive behaviors to avoid confrontation.

5. Blaming Outside Factors – Saying things like, "They drink because work is stressful," instead of holding them accountable.

6. Feeling Responsible for Their Happiness – Trying to "fix" their problems instead of letting them deal with consequences.

ADD TO YOUR DICTIONARY
Codependent
Enabling
Enmeshed
Family dynamic

THE IMPACT OF ENABLING

- Prevents personal growth and accountability.
- Keeps the enabler in a cycle of stress and exhaustion.
- Can worsen addiction, irresponsibility, or toxic behaviors.
- Creates unhealthy dynamics in relationships.

Generational Assessment

AREA	DEPENDENCE & INDEPENDENCE
Are women taught to be independent or dependent?	
Is your mom/daughter dependent or independent?	
Has control become toxic with your mom or daughter?	

JOURNAL PROMPTS: DEPENDENCE & INDEPENDENCE

1. What kind of responsibilities did your mom have? Was she overwhelmed with activities, volunteer work, family, a job? List them.

2. Which of her struggles and challenges were you aware of? Which weren't you aware of?

3. How much independence did you have?

4. Does your mom/daughter have control issues? Around what?

5. What are your conversations or fights like around these issues?

6. Codependence is emotional reliance on someone else. Have you noticed you and your mother are too closely connected? What does that look like?

UPDATING "MY STORY"

Time to add this new information to your mother-daughter story. Start this section of your story off with a heading titled something like: What I Didn't Know about codependency and enabling.

CHAPTER 15
BOUNDARIES & DETACHMENT

Reading Assignment: Chapter 11 of *The Mother Daughter Relationship Makeover* page 153

So many conflicts between moms and daughters result from lack of boundaries. These are behavior guidelines. These days it may seem that behavior guidelines have been abandoned. People feel free to rage at each other over their differences rather than work together to find solutions. Civility and compassion go out the window.

Every family creates its own relationship rules. We talked about the characteristics of healthy and toxic friendships. The same thing applies in family relationships. Boundaries can establish emotional kindness and physical safety as we pointed out. Boundaries are especially essential in mother-daughter relationships because they create a healthy balance between closeness and individuality. Without clear boundaries, the relationship can become overly enmeshed, or distant. Healthy boundaries allow both mother and daughter to feel respected, heard, and emotionally secure so let's learn them.

TYPES OF BOUNDARIES

- **Physical** - "I'm not as touchy feely as you so please don't invade my space like that."

- **Intellectual** - "It's fine that we don't agree on this issue but please respect my belief."

- **Financial and Material** - "No, you can't borrow my new dress, I haven't worn it yet."

- **Emotional** - "I appreciate your advice, but I need to make my own decisions."

- **Time** - "I can't talk every day, but let's schedule a weekly call."

- **Privacy** - "I need space in my relationships and don't want to discuss every detail."

- **Respect** - "Please don't criticize my parenting/appearance/choices—I need support, not judgment."

EXAMPLES OF BOUNDARIES

Physical Boundaries relate to your body and personal space, which may include your home. Sending the message that a mom/daughter can come anytime may invite more invasion than is tolerable. Sending a message that a mom/daughter can come at certain times when you're free sets a boundary that creates autonomy in your own home. Setting boundaries can also include what can and must not be removed from your home or changed in your home. Parents have the right to set these boundaries, but so do adult daughters. Physical boundaries can also include too much touching or hugging that makes you uncomfortable and anxious. Leslie remembers her mom forcing her to kiss and hug distant relations she didn't know. Ugh. Too much advice may set you on edge. Don't eat this. Don't eat that. Your body is yours. It's important to take care of your body, but only you are in control of what you want and what you should do.

Intellectual Boundaries are all about your ideas, thoughts, beliefs, and spiritual life. No one has the right to impose their beliefs on you. This is where families disagree and don't always respect each other's opinions. We'd hazard a guess that you have a wide variety of non matching ideas, traditions, and practices in your family, like we do. Boundaries around what you should say to those who don't agree with you are important. Do you want to promote healthy self-esteem and goodwill? Then don't go on about hot-button subjects and get abusive when your mom/daughter doesn't agree with you. Things people say can have a lasting impact. You never forget the names your loved ones call you when you have your own opinions. Moms and daughters have strong feelings about most things. Boundaries help keep us safe.

Financial and Material Boundaries are about what's mine and what's yours when it comes to possessions and money. We all should be able to agree about this but rarely do. Let's clarify what belongs to you and what belongs to your mom. This is our credo for both moms and daughters. If I earned it or inherited it, it's mine. If you earned or inherited, or won the lottery or a lawsuit, it's yours. Items in your home are yours. Your clothes and bank accounts are yours. Finances are so emotional, however, that you can stay furious forever if boundaries are not set about who is in control of the finances and the possessions as well as the future of the possessions.

CREATING FINANCIAL AND MATERIAL BOUNDARIES

This is not always easy to accomplish, especially if mom has been generous throughout daughter's growing years. We know a mom, Cindy, who felt she had to give up her vacations to send her grandchildren to expensive summer camps. Fair? She didn't think so, but didn't dare say no because she feared backlash. We know many moms who stop taking care of themselves because they feel they have to help daughters who have not yet learned that money doesn't grow on trees. How can you improve this in your family? You can ask your mom how she's doing.

If your mother/daughter expects financial aid, your clothes, jewelry, credit cards, trips to Tahiti, education, and weddings for her and her children and so much more, you can set the boundaries. What can I afford to give you? What am I comfortable giving you? What don't I want you to have? No, you don't have the right to my safety deposit box or the deed on my house. So, here's where you sit down and ask yourself the questions about what you want so you can be clear about your wants and needs.

Emotional Boundaries are necessary to keep you feeling safe. You may have to learn how to create the space you need from the demands of others. Do you have a mom/daughter who calls you day and night and wants you to listen to every mood and struggle she has? Also, every snippet of gossip and happiness? Is problem-dumping the bane of your mother-daughter relationship? Listening too much will sap your energy. Especially if you are expected to respond. Even long text chains can be challenging to your patience. How much listening can you tolerate? How much support can you give? How much do you want to share about your own life and struggles? This is where emotional boundaries come in.

Time Boundaries are closely related to emotional boundaries because someone you love to the moon and back may be taking too much of your time. Time and emotional space are your most precious possessions. Time may, in fact, be everything. Say you don't argue about food or finances or beliefs, but there is a constant stream of requests for your help to run out and pick up groceries or babysit or get that resume polished, or (God forbid) do the laundry.

Do the requests for your time include work-related tasks where you help with fulfillment but don't receive financial remuneration for your contribution? Everything you do for someone else takes up your time. Boundaries in the time category can be an agreement to provide a certain number of hours a week or a day. Only a specified number of phone calls. And you split proceeds when you do a work project together. Here is where both mom and daughter are working together to make the relationship fair for everyone.

DETACHMENT

Detachment is emotional letting go. And there are many kinds of letting go. Moms must detach a thousand different ways almost every day. It's not easy to let go of fear. Moms are challenged to let go of their fears when their daughters don't eat enough, or thrive on risky activities, or invite conflict. What if they don't do their homework, or dress funny, or fail a test? What if daughters don't have friends, or have bad friends? Or have learning disabilities or other challenges moms can't fix. When a mom can't detach from fear of consequences, she risks being a nag, a total controller, from her daughter's point of view, even the enemy.

For moms with addict daughters, detachment is especially difficult because fear of the ultimate loss is not just imagined, it's very real. And there is trauma every time the phone rings. Detachment here can literally save your life. No mom is responsible for the life and death of adult children or children who are no longer living with them. Each adult has her own path, and detachment from fear creates a healthy boundary that allows both moms and daughters the opportunity to be in charge of their own lives.

Generational Assessment

AREA	BOUNDARIES
Do you and your mom/daughter have healthy boundaries? Explain	
What kind of boundaries do you want/need with your mother/daughter	
Have you ever had to detach from someone?	

JOURNAL PROMPTS: BOUNDARIES & DETACHMENT

1. Do you think your time and feelings are important? Please explain.

2. Is there anything you get stuck doing that you don't want to do? What is it?

3. With whom do you discuss your needs? Tell us about your support team.

4. After reading this chapter, what kinds of boundaries do you think you need?

5. What boundaries do you have in place?

6. In what areas do you need to put boundaries in place? Be honest.

UPDATING "MY STORY"

Time to add this new information to your mother-daughter story. Start this section of your story off with a heading titled something like 'What I Didn't Know about boundaries and detachment.

ADD TO YOUR DICTIONARY

Boundaries

Detachment

"LOVE YOURSELF ENOUGH TO SAY NO TO OTHERS' DEMANDS ON YOUR TIME AND ENERGY."

– BARBARA DE ANGELIS

CHAPTER 16
ALCOHOL & DRUGS

Reading Assignment: Chapter 12 of *The Mother Daughter Relationship Makeover* page 165

Mothers who abuse alcohol or drugs can put daughters into danger in more ways than we can document here. Real danger from exposure to drugs at home to dangerous situations coupled with lack of stability and inadequate parenting create lasting emotional consequences for daughters. Moms in active addiction are not able to manage daily caretaking tasks and may have wildly changing emotional ups and downs.

By the same token, daughters who struggle with addiction or alcoholism make life for moms a rollercoaster of emotions that range between extreme worry and profound anger. Let's unpack what alcoholism and addiction can do to the mother-daughter relationship.

Alcohol and drugs can create significant conflict by eroding trust, increasing emotional instability, and shifting family dynamics. Whether the mother, daughter, or both struggle with substance use, addiction can cause deep emotional pain, miscommunication, and codependency. Here's how it impacts the relationship:

Breakdown of Trust

- **Lies & Secrecy:** Substance abuse always leads to dishonesty—hiding drinking/drug use, sneaking around, or making false promises you want to keep but can't.

- **Unreliability:** If your mom or daughter is frequently intoxicated or in withdrawal, they will cancel plans, forget commitments, or fail to be emotionally present.

Emotional Distance & Resentment

- **Neglect & Emotional Unavailability:** A mother struggling with addiction may not provide the emotional support a daughter needs, leading to feelings of abandonment.

- **Role Reversal:** If a daughter has to take care of an addicted mother, she may feel burdened with responsibility, leading to resentment.

Increased Conflict & Tension

- **Irritability & Mood Swings:** Substance use can cause erratic behavior, making arguments more frequent and unpredictable.

- **Guilt & Shame:** A mother may feel ashamed of her addiction and push her daughter away, or a daughter struggling with substance use may feel judged and rebel.

Codependency & Enabling

- **Mothers Enabling Daughters:** Some mothers may financially or emotionally enable their daughter's addiction by making excuses, covering up, or providing money.

- **Daughters Enabling Mothers:** Daughters may protect their mothers from consequences, leading to an unhealthy cycle where addiction is not confronted.

Generational Trauma & Cycles of Addiction

- **Trauma Passed From Mothers:** When mothers struggle with substance abuse, daughters may develop unhealthy coping mechanisms or even turn to substances herself.
- **Why Past Traumas Need To Be Addressed:** Without addressing the root issues, addiction can become a repeated pattern in the family.

HOW ALCOHOLISM AFFECTS THE MOTHER-DAUGHTER RELATIONSHIP

Here are a few of the issues that can arise from having an alcoholic mother: anxiety, fears of abandonment, difficulty forming attachments in adult relationships, emotional dysregulation. And here are a few issues that can arise from having an alcoholic child: becoming an enabler, trying to fix or control, extreme obsession over the alcoholic, losing the ability to care for yourself.

SIGNS AND SYMPTOMS OF ALCOHOLISM AND ADDICTION

Increased tolerance; trouble stopping; harmed relationships; unreliable, dangerous behavior (driving drunk, reckless sexual behavior); spending lots of time drinking or recovering from drinking; inability to stop drinking despite efforts to regulate or cut down; cravings; obsession over the next high; change in behavior/eating habits/friends; losing interest in school or work; trouble

Generational Assessment

AREA	ALCOHOL AND DRUGS
Does your family drink alcohol, abuse drugs?	
Does your mom/daughter drink too much?	
Does your mom/daughter take drugs that scare you?	
Is the family concerned about drinking and drugging?	
Has alcoholism or addiction impacted your mother-daughter relationship?	

JOURNAL PROMPTS: ALCOHOL AND DRUGS

Please note: we have many resources on how to manage or detach from an alcoholic or addict mother or daughter. Please see **Reachoutrecovery.com** for articles, resources, books and worksheets. You can also check out our Youtube series on parenting at ***www.youtube.com/@reachoutrecovery6052.***

This can be hard to write. Imagine this mom and daughter who have not gotten this honest about our lives until right now. So we know how difficult and painful it is to explore your experiences with drugs and alcohol. Here we want you to explore the real estate that alcohol and drugs have had in your life and your emotions. How have they affected both your mother-daughter relationship and your own emotional well-being? We can bet that you have some scars that you don't even know about or know about and pretend they didn't happen. It's okay to think and write about them here. This is your story, and you can tell it now.

1. How do you use alcohol and/or drugs? (Socially, to feel better, etc.) Describe your use.

2. Do you worry about your drug or alcohol use? Please explain.

3. Do you worry about your mother's /daughter's drug or alcohol use? Please explain.

4. What changes do you want to make around your drinking?

5. If you worry about your drinking or substance abuse, have you ever tried to stop? What happened?

6. If you worry about your mother's/daughter's drinking, have you ever tried to talk to her? How did that go?

UPDATING "MY STORY"

Time to add this new information to your mother-daughter story. Start this section of your story off with a heading titled something like 'What I Didn't Know About Alcoholism And My Mom/Daughter.

ADD TO YOUR DICTIONARY

Addiction

Sobriety

Emotional sobriety

Alcoholism

Drug or alcohol tolerance

Alcohol & Drugs

ALCOHOL SELF-ASSESSMENT: IS DRINKING HELPING OR HURTING?

It's easy to get in the habit of daily drinking without realizing the impact it's having on your life. If you are dealing with stress at work, at home, or anywhere, alcohol can become an easily accessible stress-reliever. But, sometimes, the alcohol ends up becoming more of a problem than a solution. This quick self-assessment is designed to help you see whether your drinking is truly casual or beginning to affect your mood, relationships, and your mother-daughter bond.

Instructions:
Read each statement below and check the box if it applies to you. Be truthful, this is for your reflection, not judgment.

REFLECTION

If you checked 0-2 boxes: Alcohol may not be having a major effect right now, but stay aware of how it shows up in your life.

If you checked 3-5 boxes: Drinking is beginning to impact your well-being and relationships. Consider exploring healthier coping strategies and support.

If you checked 6 or more boxes: Alcohol may be causing significant harm. Reaching out for help—from a trusted friend, therapist, or support group—can make a powerful difference.

Remember: The key here is awareness. With clarity comes the ability to make informed decisions on how to carry forward. This is only meant to help you see if alcohol is helping you or creating new issues.

ALCOHOL USE CHECKLIST

- ☐ I sometimes drink more than I intend to once I start.
- ☐ I've missed work, school, or important responsibilities because of drinking, or recovering from drinking.
- ☐ My drinking has caused arguments or tension with family, friends, or my partner.
- ☐ I've used alcohol to cope with stress, sadness, or anxiety.
- ☐ I've been told by others that I drink too much, or I hide how much I drink.
- ☐ I feel guilty or regretful about things I said or did while drinking.
- ☐ I need more alcohol than I used to in order to feel its effects.
- ☐ I've skipped meals, sleep, or self-care routines because of drinking.
- ☐ My moods feel more unstable, anxious, or depressed when I drink.
- ☐ I've tried to cut down or stop drinking, but found it hard to do so.

CHAPTER 17
MENTAL ILLNESS

Reading Assignment: Chapter 13 of *The Mother Daughter Relationship Makeover* page 181

The fear of behavior differences and mental illnesses goes way back. This is one of the secrets and lies that haunts every family. We all have peculiar, difficult, and downright weird members of our family. They may act weird, have strange thoughts, or can't function at all. There are family members who have phobias (extreme fears), who have depression, who have psychotic episodes where they are not connected with reality. We also have aging family members with memory loss. These are all forms of mental health challenges. Not to mention personality issues and disorders.

But let's just think about the term mental health for a moment. Mental health is just like physical health in the sense that it's neutral. Just like with physical health where many things can go wrong, mental health is variable. Mental health changes with positive and negative experiences, trauma and physical damage and injuries. Into all lives some bad things are going to happen. And you can be born with neurological differences that cause behavioral challenges.

HERE ARE SIX COMMON MENTAL ILLNESSES

- Obsessive-compulsive disorder, and phobias.
- Depression, bipolar disorder, and other mood disorders.
- Eating disorders.
- Personality disorders.
- Post-traumatic stress disorder (PTSD)
- Psychotic disorders, including schizophrenia.

We would also add addiction to that list as well as those we mentioned above: some character and personality disorders. Everyone is affected by the mental health of those around them. Here are just a few examples of how healthy people can experience a mental illness at some time in their life and then affect everyone in their family dynamic.

- A veteran returning from military service who has to readjust to civilian life.
- A healthy teen who is bullied or has experienced a sexual assault.
- A new mom who has postpartum depression.
- A middle aged mom who is overwhelmed by the loss of a job or a home or a marriage.
- Any mom who is coping with the addiction of her children.
- A daughter who has to care for her elderly mom with dementia while managing her job and family.
- A teen daughter who has to take responsibility for the family because her mom is absent.
- Moms and daughters facing deportation or separation.

These are just a few of millions of situations that cause stress, trauma, and mental health challenges that change the family dynamic. Let's add the attention-deficit/hyperactivity disorder (ADHD) to the list. ADHD is one of the most common mental disorders affecting children. But coping with illnesses of any kind creates emotional stresses on moms that can lead to depression and physical symptoms as well.

MOTHER-DAUGHTER MENTAL HEALTH CONNECTION

Mothers who are struggling with mental health challenges tend to struggle with taking care of themselves and their daughters. The risks to daughters living with a mother with untreated mental illness go beyond neglect. These daughters are exposed to instability, frightening events, and a complete lack of emotional and physical support. Their basic needs aren't met. If there is abuse in the home, the chances of these daughters growing up to struggle with self-esteem issues, substance abuse issues, or untreated mental illness skyrocket.

SIGNS AND SYMPTOMS OF MENTAL ILLNESS

- Feeling sadness more than usual.
- Excessive fears or worries or extreme feelings of guilt.
- Extreme mood changes of highs and lows.
- Withdrawal from friends and activities.
- Feeling more confused.
- Significant tiredness, low energy.
- Problems sleeping.
- Change in eating habits.
- Detachment from reality (delusions), paranoia, or hallucinations.
- Inability to cope with daily problems or stress.
- Trouble relating to situations and to people.
- Alcohol and drug use increase.
- Sex drive changes.
- Excessive anger, hostility or violence.
- Suicidal thinking.

THINK ABOUT THIS

Mental illness can affect us and our families in ways we don't necessarily think about. Learning the family mental health history can be helpful in this journey of self-discovery and relationship makeover. Realizing who in the family may have struggled with a mental health issue and whether your mother/daughter may be battling something you didn't realize is enlightening. For many, accepting a mental health issue and seeking treatment is the beginning of a much happier, less dramatic life.

Generational Assessment

AREA	MENTAL HEALTH
Is it accepted in your culture to discuss mental health?	
Has your economics affected yours/your mom's mental health?	
Does your mom or daughter try to manage your mental health?	
Is mental health a problem in your family?	

TIME TO JOURNAL

Here we want you to think about how mental health has affected your family and you. Is it a topic you feel comfortable talking about at home? Does your family have shame around this issue, and how has that affected you? The goal here is to find understanding and compassion so we can support each other.

JOURNAL PROMPTS: MENTAL HEALTH

Please note: we have many resources on how to manage or detach from a mother or daughter who is dealing with mental health issues. Please see **Reachoutrecovery.com** for articles, resources, books and worksheets.

1. Are you aware of any mental illness in your family? Please explain.

2. What mental health issues did you see growing up with mom or yourself?

3. Did she receive treatment? If not, why not?

4. Was mental health discussed in your family? If not, why not?

5. Have you ever experienced a mental health issue? What happened?

6. Are you and your mother on the same page about mental health issues?

Mental Illness

Each of the areas is deeply personal and until you take the time to explore the 'whys' they will not be resolved. The Journal Prompts at the end of each chapter will help you to dig deeper into these issues. Is there an area we did not mention? If so, add it to your personal chart.

UPDATING "MY STORY"

Time to add this new information to your mother-daughter story. Start this section of your story off with a heading titled something like 'What I Didn't Know!'

LEARNING ACTIVITIES

EIGHT AREAS FOR POTENTIAL CONFLICT

After reading through the information provided for each area, use this chart to rank the eight areas. What is your #1 area of conflict?
Be specific. For example, if Appearance and Style is the #1 area in your mother-daughter relationship that really pushes your buttons, think about why. It can be a power issue: "You will not leave this house looking like a tramp." Or it can be a shame issue: "That dress makes you look 10 pounds heavier. And that color does nothing for you." It can be a need to express individuality: "I am wearing this because I LIKE IT!"

Please rank your most challenging issues from 1 to 8
- Food and Weight
- Finances and Money
- Appearance and Style
- Friends and Romandic partners
- Dependence and Independence
- Boundaries and Detachment
- Alcohol and Drugs
- Mental Health

AREA	WHY I RANKED IT

"YOU ARE NOT ALONE IN YOUR STRUGGLES, EVEN IF IT FEELS THAT WAY."
– EMBRACE HEALTH

CHAPTER 18
STEP 3: TRIGGERS, TRAUMA, & CONFLICT RESOLUTION

Reading Assignment: Chapter 14 of *The Mother Daughter Relationship Makeover* page 197

Simply put, an emotional trigger is a stimulus that launches a positive or negative emotional reaction. It all happens pretty unconsciously in your brain. For our purposes we will focus on negative triggers. For example, the smell of garbage could remind you of a hoarder parent who didn't take the garbage out. For someone trying to stay sober, the smell of a bar could make you want to drink. Suddenly, you're uncomfortable, anxious and your brain wants you to respond in some way to keep you safe. Even if you are safe.

The biology of the brain is explained more deeply in the *Mother Daughter Relationship Makeover.* Brain biology is important because your moods, motivation, and judgment are all controlled by your limbic cortex. This is a part of the brain that reacts to emotion, not reason or experience. Surprisingly, it's not until we are solidly in our twenties before the limbic system is considered fully developed, and we can use reason to control our moods and reaction.. Of course, if you have not learned how to regulate your reactions and responses, it doesn't matter what age you are. Self-regulation is a learned skill.

SELF-REGULATION AND TRIGGERS

Self-regulation is essential in dealing with triggers because moms and daughters 'trigger' each other all the time. A trigger may be a certain facial expression that shows frustration, disdain, or a mumbled, "Not that again!" Whatever the trigger, it enrages or humiliates you immediately. Triggers can make you go from 0 to 100 in a second. Your blood boils, your pulse quickens and you want to react. That is a physical reaction and was the cause of so many fights for us.

Our big issues were around food, control, sobriety, and mental health. Imagine that just a quick critical glance at what one of us was eating could start a fight. Anything that brought out issues of control or blame around alcoholism would put either one of us through the roof. This is why it's so important to understand what your areas of conflict are so you can see how easily you get triggered when they come up. Triggers need to be acknowledged and managed.

SO WHAT DOES GETTING TRIGGERED FEEL LIKE

You know it when it happens, your mom or daughter walks in with a wretched expression on her face and immediately launches into a criticism of some kind. Within .00001 seconds you're angry or hurt, your heartbeat increases, you might feel hot all over, some people even shake or panic when they're triggered. And, the undeniable outcome? Reacting defensively, becoming enraged and feeling completely overwhelmed. Now, suddenly you're in defense mode and probably yelling and exacerbating a panicked and unhealthy reaction. Is it your fault? Absolutely not, but knowledge is power and once you know what this feeling is, you have the power to stop it.

SYMPTOMS OF BEING TRIGGERED

If you're not sure when you're being triggered, try breaking it down by these symptoms.

Emotional
Do you have emotional symptoms like sudden rage, panic, or overwhelming sadness? What about anxiety or dread that

feels disproportionate to the situation? Feeling rejected, abandoned, or shamed are also common emotional symptoms to being triggered. Numbness or emotional shutdown can also happen for some people.

Physical
The physical symptoms are often the easiest to recognize. You're triggered and suddenly your heart is racing, you might shake, sweat or even feel nausea. Lindsey has those. Whether it's a panic attack or something frightens her, she will shake, sweat and feel sick for a few minutes. The struggle is real, know that. In very serious cases, you may have trouble breathing, get totally fatigued or even feel "frozen."

Cognitive
Cognitive symptoms were the ones we worked the hardest to heal because for us, they were the most destructive. Cognitive symptoms are in your head–the floods of negative thinking like, "I'm not good enough or no one cares." You can experience intrusive thoughts or memories, flashbacks to bad or uncomfortable moments in your life, and it can be difficult to concentrate. Other features are a lack of memory or very black and white thinking.

Behavioral
Behavioral symptoms are the most dangerous, in our opinion. This is where your behavior can radically disrupt your life and the lives of others - no bueno. Behavioral symptoms include, lashing out (or withdrawing) from others, escapism behavior like drinking, substances, screens, food, love/sex addiction, gambling, or even riskier behaviors like self-harm or putting yourself in dangerous situations. You can also find the people-pleasers, codependents, and avoidants in this group.

TYPES OF TRIGGERS

External Triggers: When the World Pushes a Button
External triggers are things happening outside of us that stir up emotional reactions. These can include:

- Critical tone of voice.
- A particular word or phrase ("You're being too sensitive").
- Judgmental looks.
- Slamming doors or the silent treatment.
- Important dates or places.

In mother-daughter relationships, external triggers often show up in repeating patterns. For example, if a daughter hears her mom ask, "Are you really going to wear that?" it might not be just about clothes—it might trigger old wounds about not feeling accepted or good enough. Similarly, a mother might hear her daughter say, "You never listen," and instantly feel unappreciated or attacked—especially if she's carrying her own unhealed hurt from the past.

Internal Triggers: When the Pain Comes From Yourself
Internal triggers are more subtle—and often more powerful. These are the emotional reactions that arise from our own thoughts, beliefs, and past experiences. They can be stirred up even when nothing is "wrong." Examples include:

- Constantly feeling "less than."
- Feeling like everyone is disappointed in me or I've let her down.
- Shame, guilt, shame, guilt.

In mother-daughter relationships, internal triggers are often tied to childhood memories, unmet needs, or family patterns passed down for generations. A mom may feel triggered by her daughter's independence—not because it's wrong, but because it unconsciously reminds her of how she wasn't allowed to be independent. A daughter might feel triggered by her mother's concern, interpreting it as control—because she's still carrying the belief that love always comes with strings attached.

MOTHER-DAUGHTER TRIGGERS

There are some universal triggers for moms and daughters that have been around since the beginning of time, and they will come as no surprise.

Rejection. No one likes rejection, but rejection from a mother or daughter cuts like a knife. Whether it's a major rejection that created real trauma or little rejections here and there that cause a lack of self-esteem, rejection in the mother-daughter relationship can be very toxic.

Criticism. Anyone who has/had a critical mom or deals with a critical daughter knows all too well the damage constant criticism can do to your mental health and sense of self. Mom and daughter are supposed to be there to make you feel good and supported, right? Funny, how many mothers and daughters get in the criticism habit and don't see anything wrong with it.

Shaming and blaming. Shame and blame are bad enough when they come from other people in the world but when they come from your mom or daughter, they create soul hurt.

Nagging/Tone of Voice. Whether it's a frustrated mom snapping, "Are you wearing that again?" or a tantrum-y daughter complaining that she doesn't like dinner when mom is tired and has been working all day - nagging and tone of voice can be the most common triggers.

Oversharing. A mom or daughter who shares absolutely everything whether it's appropriate or not can be destructive. A daughter doesn't need to know everything about mom's marriage and friends even though the desire to be friends is strong.

Patterns of Conflict. At this point, you've spent some time thinking, and hopefully writing, about your top issues with mom or daughter in step two. Now, you have some concept of how these issues turn into triggers. From there, can you see some patterns? The patterns of conflict are the key to resolving them.

LEARNING ACTIVITIES

DEVELOPING AN EFFECTIVE SELF-REGULATION PLAN FOR DEALING WITH TRIGGERS

Triggers don't just disappear. You must consciously identify them (self-awareness), try to figure out the cause (deeper self-awareness), and then find tools and strategies that you can use to diffuse the triggers (making effective decisions).

SOME TOOLS AND STRATEGIES TO EXPLORE:

Identifying the Emotional Response – Use journaling to help you gain clarity on what your triggers are and how they started. Keep some sentence frames handy to help you process the trigger response.

Step 1 - Identify the action and the response.

When _____ (person) says or does _____ (action), my immediate response is _____ .
I noticed _____ (symptom) happens when _____ (person) says or does _____ (action).

Step 2 – Try to figure out why you react the way you do.

I always _____ (what is your immediate reaction?) because _____ (why?). This reaction results in me _____ (talking back, rolling my eyes, walking out). Why have I never considered _____ (a new action).

Step 3 – Choose a healthier option for responding.

Do a quick body scan to find where in your body this trigger is causing a response. Immediately begin controlled deep breathing. Practice a key phrase that will allow you to control the situation such as, "This is not healthy for me. I am not talking about this right now."

The more you identify your triggers, locate the cause, and prepare a more effective response, the more mentally and physically healthier you will become.

JOURNAL PROMPTS: TRIGGERS

1. What are your areas of sensitivity or triggers?

2. Can you remember when and where they started? Take some time and go back to an incident that created the trigger. Explain it as well as you can.

3. What does being triggered feel like to you? Where in your body do you react to the trigger? What emotions does the trigger cause?

4. What happens when you try to talk to your mom/daughter about your feelings?

5. What would you like to change? Do you want peace, an apology, reassurance?

ADDITIONAL RESOURCES:

Glass, Leslie. *Teen Guide to Health: How to be your best self: Physical Emotional and Social.* Chapter Six: Brains: Teen VS Adult & Stages of Growth

Glass, Lindsey *100 Tips for Growing Up: My 20 Years of Recovery*

www.ReachOutRecovery.com

CHAPTER 19
TRAUMA

Reading Assignment: Chapter 15 of *The Mother Daughter Relationship Makeover* page 213

UNDERSTANDING TRAUMA

Trauma is a lasting emotional response to a stressful event that can cause physical, emotional, and/or life-threatening harm. Trauma is an event that causes long-term mental or emotional damage, or an injury to the body. Trauma has no boundaries regarding age, gender, socioeconomic status, race, ethnicity, or sexual orientation. Examples of trauma inducing events include accidents, wars, crimes, natural disasters, abuse, neglect, witnessing violence, or the death of a loved one. However not all trauma is easy to define. Often traumatic events are hidden because of shame or threat of retribution. Trauma is a complex and challenging issue.

It is easy to see why trauma is a part of the mother-daughter relationship. Even mothers and daughters in healthy relationships have experienced trauma. It just adds more challenges to a struggling mother-daughter relationship.

There are three types of traumas: acute, chronic, and complex. Read this and make a list of traumatic events in your life in your journal so you can return to them as you read this chapter. Remember that not all traumatic events are the BIG ones like surviving multiple wildfires or a school shooting (which one of us has experienced), but the daily traumas we encounter all impact our mental, physical, and spiritual well-being. The math teacher who always called on boys first during your algebra class created a chronic trauma for you as a girl. The message was clear.

TYPES OF TRAUMA

- **Acute:** Results from a single incident. A car accident, natural disaster, school shooting, or violent sexual attack are examples.

- **Chronic:** The trauma happens repeatedly. Bullying, cyberbullying, domestic violence, sexual harassment, sexual abuse, food insecurity, homelessness, and addiction are some forms of chronic trauma.

- **Complex:** Ongoing and multiple exposures to several different kinds of trauma. The child/family who must relocate every few years due to lack of employment or conflict and violence, social injustice and discrimination from social status and discriminatory laws, gender discrimination that limits educational opportunities are a few.

- **Female Trauma:** Biological and psychological incidents contributing to stress that impact all women include reproductive health, how sexuality and sexual reproduction were presented to you as a young person, period management from monthly menstruating, access or lack of to hygiene products, hormonal changes, fertility issues, pregnancy, rape, miscarriages, and more.

ADD TO YOUR DICTIONARY

Triggers

Trauma

Generational Trauma

Symptoms
Symptoms can include shock, denial, unpredictable emotions, flashbacks, strained relationships, headaches, nausea, and more. We'll discuss more below.

Impact
Trauma can harm a person's sense of safety, self, and ability to regulate emotions. People with trauma may feel shame, helplessness, powerlessness, and intense fear.

Personal
What's traumatic is personal, and different people can react to the same experience differently or for longer.

Risk factors
Some groups are more likely to experience trauma than others, including people of color, people who have served in the military, people who are in prison, refugees, and asylum seekers.

UNDERSTANDING MOTHER-DAUGHTER RELATIONSHIP TRAUMA

Mother-daughter trauma isn't always about one defining, dramatic event. Sometimes, it's the quiet, repeated emotional wounds that leave the deepest marks—feeling unloved, or love that feels conditional, impossible expectations that shaped how we see ourselves, the resentment from having to care for a mother instead of being cared for, or caring far too long for a daughter who won't grow up. All of these, and many other situations can create pain and wounds.

Common Examples:
- Never feeling seen or emotionally nurtured.
- Chronic shaming or guilting.
- Total fear of speaking your mind because of negative or shaming reactions.
- Never being good enough.
- Chronic judgment or being dismissed.
- Serious control issues.
- Neglectful parenting.
- Alcoholism, addiction, or mental illness.

What's even worse, this trauma can be passed down through generations like an emotional inheritance; and this is known as generational trauma. A mother who never felt safe to express her needs may raise a daughter who never feels worthy of hers. A daughter who grew up walking on eggshells may become a woman who doubts her voice, even in safe spaces. This type of trauma doesn't always show in the ways you would expect. It manifests in quiet patterns of control that no one talks about. It lives in the emotional issues, or distance, or anxiety that flows through the family. It's a grandmother who endured abuse but never processed it—so now the family tiptoes around conflict like it's life or death. It's perfectionism. Codependency. Hyper-independence. Rage that shows up at the worst times—or the inability to feel much at all.

Other examples of generational or ancestral trauma include: living through a war, poverty, cultural discrimination against gender, ethnic cleansing, abuse, sexual abuse, untreated mental illness.

TRAUMA SURVIVOR SYMPTOMS

If your next question is, how do I know if I have unhealed trauma, then ask yourself do I have any of the following?

- Trouble regulating emotions.
- Inability to form close partnerships.
- Impulsivity.
- Nightmares.
- Anxiety.
- Intrusive thoughts.
- Memory loss.
- Isolating.
- Changing routines to feel safe.

Other Mother-Daughter Trauma You May Have Experienced

- Childbirth/loss.
- Death.
- Divorce.
- Abandonment.
- Job loss.
- Abusive or mentally ill father or family member.
- Constant relocation.
- Financial instability.

In Step 4, we delve deep into healing and forgiveness so we won't get into that now, but we do want to mention TIP's because these are ways to begin to support your mother/daughter if she's been through trauma, or how to think about asking for help for yourself.

TRAUMA INFORMED PRACTICES (TIPS)

Trauma-informed practices are methods to support people who have experienced trauma or toxic stress. They are based on the idea that trauma can affect a person's health, relationships, and behaviors. Healing from trauma is possible, but often requires professional guidance.

TRAUMA-INFORMED PRACTICES AIM TO:

Reduce stigma: Help reduce the stigma around mental health disorders, substance use, and other effects of trauma.
Show empathy: Understand and share the feelings of others.
Provide support: Offer services and support that uplift and don't blame the person.

Create a strength-based approach: Highlight how common it is for trauma to be present in certain behaviors and symptoms.

Promote safety: Ensure that staff and the people they serve feel physically and psychologically safe.

Foster collaboration: Encourage people to share responsibility for achieving a common goal.

Promote empowerment: Give people power and control over their own lives.

Consider cultural issues: Take cultural, historical, and gender issues into account.

Some principles of trauma-informed care include:
- Creating trustworthiness and transparency.
- Building a community of peer support and mutual self-help.
- Empowering, voice, and choice.

The trauma-informed approach is guided by four assumptions, known as the "Four R's."
- Realization about trauma and how it can affect people and groups.
- Recognizing the signs of trauma.
- Having a system that can respond to trauma.
- Resisting re-traumatization.

CONTINUING "MY STORY"
Return to your ongoing story of your mother-daughter relationship. You have just explored a significant source of tension and conflict in your relationship. How does this new knowledge reframe your story? What can you do with the new knowledge to help create a healthier mother-daughter relationship?

LEARNING ACTIVITIES

CONNECTING THE DOTS
What are the trauma events that impacted or are impacting your mother-daughter relationship? For example, how did each of you learn about the menstrual cycle? Did you feel supported in this coming-of-age event or was it a total surprise? Did mom hand you a brochure and tell you where the hygiene products are kept or was there a conversation about what it means and what to expect?

Take some time to reflect on the mother-daughter related traumas you have experienced individually and then how they inform your relationship. If you can share this information, do you and your mom both remember it the same way? Where are the points that are not the same and why? Your trauma may not be her trauma. Discuss the whys.

JOURNAL PROMPTS : TRAUMA

1. Explore trauma in your family. Are you aware of any trauma in your family history?

2. Has your mother or grandmother had experiences that have affected them in traumatic ways? (They may not think of some events as traumatic – but immigrating from another country, being a non-English speaker, not having a family support system are all trauma-inducing life events.)

3. Are/were there divorces in your family? Divorce is a major trauma event, even if it is amicable.

4. How has reproductive health been a traumatic experience for your mom or grandmother? Have they ever talked about it or is it not openly discussed?

CHAPTER 20
TECHNIQUES TO KEEP THE PEACE

Reading Assignment: Chapter 16 of *The Mother Daughter Relationship Makeover* page 233

DID YOU SEE PATTERNS OF CONFLICT

As we are about to get into conflict resolution tools, are you clear on where you might be able to implement them? We want to teach you new communication methods and how to pause when agitated, but you must know when and how your conflict arises. As we delve into resolution, consider exactly when you will need these tools so you're prepared. One way we set ourselves up for success is to expect bumps along the way. When you can anticipate the fight happening, you'll be ready to diffuse.

WHERE DO YOUR FEELINGS GET TRIGGERED

Whether it's an emotional, physical or behavioral reaction, has learning about triggers and trauma helped you identify yours? We want you to be reaching for these new techniques the minute you feel one of those trigger symptoms rise up. It's hardest to remember what to do when we are overcome by emotion or fear or anger and want to react, rage, or drink. So, prepare for the fight and prepare for the trigger symptom because that's when you need to change course.

HEALTHIER COMMUNICATION

When you start to change your relationship with someone you used to have conflict with, it's crucial to change the way you speak to them. We know it's hard to change your ways after a lifetime of unhealthy communication patterns, but your relationship will not get better if you don't alter the way you are behaving, whatever role you played in the relationship. Everyone has to change so healthy communication can reign.

TIPS TO KEEP THE PEACE

Hit Pause

Remember, peace is intentional. Especially when we have the fighting habit. We have to create peace starting with our instant reactions. The minute your mom or daughter says something, looks at you funny, or does something that would have started a fight; find your way to pause and not react. This is our adult time out.

You can step away for a few moments by excusing yourself politely to take the time you need to get back on the beam. Or, you can say something like, "Let's stop for a moment. I need to think about this before I respond," or "I don't want to respond to that at all right now."

Lindsey and Leslie often take a time out to take a few deep breaths right at that moment of instant reaction. Simply stopping the impulse to respond or rage is step one.

Then, taking a moment to clarify what you're feeling to yourself can be helpful. Instead of racing into, "I hate her, why does she do this to me," try, "I'm OK, I'm just feeling triggered. These are old feelings and I can breathe through this moment and not get upset." Again, you have more power over your mind than you think. Pause, reflect, change course. If you keep practicing this it becomes habit.

Say What You Mean Without Being Mean

How can you connect instead of disconnect? The point of healthy communication is to connect in a positive way. Here are some simple tricks that will help. For one, use "I" statements instead of "You." Do you like it when someone is constantly telling you what's wrong with you or what you're not doing right? Of course not, no one does. Start talking to your loved ones from the "I" point of view. For example instead of, "You always criticize me," try: "I feel hurt when my choices are questioned. I really need support."

Avoid the "You never," or "You always," because those statements immediately shut someone down. These statements disconnect instead of bring you together. They don't open the door to a positive response. Your goal is to get on the same page and begin feeling you're on the same team even when you don't agree.

Validation is another wonderful tool for better communication. When you validate someone else and how they are feeling, you are opening the door to connection and compassion. For example, you can say something like, "I hear that you are worried, but I need space to figure this out in my own way." Lindsey and Leslie got along much better when we were able to recognize the feelings beneath the reactions and acknowledge them.

Be emotionally honest and vulnerable without the drama. Think you can do that because nothing works better. If you can learn to tell the truth calmly and kindly, you win. It's not that you'll always receive the exact reaction you want, but you'll be able to keep your side of the street clean, metaphorically speaking.

Listen, Listen, Listen

We all want to be loved and understood and that begins with feeling heard. But, when you have a fight history, patiently listening usually went out the window years ago. That's why learning new techniques to listen so you can make them feel safe when they are speaking is an important part of this process.

The first step to becoming a good listener is to practice active listening. Active listening is listening intently with the intention of understanding what is being said to you. It does not include thinking about how to respond, judging what's being said to you, or waiting for the person to finish speaking so it's your turn. This takes practice when you have never done it before. Sometimes, you literally have to force yourself to pay attention and stop thinking about your rebuttal. In time, with practice, good listening will become intuitive.

For example, when Lindsey and Leslie had the fighting habit, there was no pause and there was no listening. Trying to get your point across was an exercise in frustration. Lindsey remembers the anxiety she had in going into any tough conversation. Without healthy communication skills, when things exploded, there was no coming back.

Instead, try listening and asking probing questions. "Mom, tell me why you feel this way. I need to understand where you are coming from." Or "I do not see it that way. Can I explain why?" Have a respectful conversation without blame or judgment. The goal is to create bridges to connections and understanding. If you find yourself getting out of control, respectfully take a break. Keep asking the important why questions. Why does she do that? Why do I react the way I do? Only you have the choice of how you react.

TIPS TO PUT THE FIRE OUT

As we keep saying, this is a process and a lifelong journey, so knowing how to de-escalate is crucial. There will be moments where disagreements will begin and that is totally to be expected so let's talk about what to do when the feelings are rising.

You know it well, what was supposed to be an easy request has turned into a heated moment where the accusations have started flying. Instead of going down that same rabbit hole, let's calm the storm because your goal is not to be right, it's to find a connection.

Identify What's Happening

The first thing you can try is to name what's happening. For example saying something like, "Whoa, this is not how I want this conversation to go. It feels like we're getting upset and talking at each other instead of to each other." See if a little awareness about the energy shift helps regulate.

Request A Time Out

If you need to take it a step further, request a time out or a moment to regroup for both of you. This is not a punishment to be clear, so don't feel like asking for one is or if someone asks you for one they're dismissing you. This is a valuable technique that allows everyone a moment to let emotions settle.

Find A Substitute For Blame

Always make sure to stay away from blame and stay in the emotion of wanting peace. For example, instead of saying, "You always interrupt me!" Try saying, "When you interrupt me, I can't get my thoughts out and I feel threatened and get defensive."

Another technique someone taught us recently is to stop and ask someone what they meant by that. Sometimes, in the moment we say things that aren't clear or we don't totally mean. By asking someone to clarify what they mean or why they said that it can be easier to get at the root of the issue or emotion.

Bring In Humor

If you happen to have the gift of humor, here's where to use it. Make a joke, lighten the mood, put your hand on your heart and sigh, do anything to get you back to shared ground. You're on the same team even when you don't agree, so remind each other that you're there to get along and make each other feel better, not worse.

LEARNING ACTIVITIES

CONTINUING "MY STORY"

Fighting, arguing, and constant conflict result in harsh feelings, feelings of insecurity, and distrust. Sometimes it takes great courage to step outside your normal response to dysfunctional communication. In your journal, consider what it would mean to your mother-daughter relationship if you took on the role of the peacekeeper. Have you ever considered it? Read through this information and reflect on what skills you would need to gain and how it could change your mother-daughter communication.

Think about what it means to be a peacekeeper.
To be a peacekeeper, you need to actively listen to different perspectives, remain neutral and impartial, practice effective communication skills, prioritize understanding others' emotions, and be willing to facilitate dialogue and compromise in conflict situations, while also being prepared to de-escalate tense moments with calmness and composure. Can you use some of the skills of a peacekeeper in your mother-daughter relationship?

Key qualities of a peacekeeper:

- **Active listening:** Pay close attention to what others are saying without interrupting and try to understand their point of view.

- **Empathy:** Try to see things from other people's perspectives and understand their emotions.

- **Non-judgmental attitude:** Avoid taking sides or making assumptions about people's intentions.

- **Effective communication:** Clearly express your own thoughts while also encouraging others to share theirs.

- **Conflict resolution skills:** Know how to mediate disagreements and find common ground between conflicting parties.

- **Calm demeanor:** Remain composed and avoid getting drawn into emotional responses during tense situations.

- **Patience:** Be willing to take the time to understand complex situations and work towards a solution.

- **Adaptability:** Be flexible and adjust your approach based on the situation and individuals involved.

How to practice being a peacekeeper:

- **Engage in dialogue:** Encourage open communication and facilitate discussion between people with different viewpoints.

- **Ask clarifying questions:** Seek to understand the underlying reasons behind conflicts and concerns.

- **Focus on common ground:** Identify areas where people agree and build on those shared interests.

- **Use "I" statements:** Express your own feelings and needs clearly without blaming others.

- **Set boundaries:** Know when to step back or seek assistance if a situation becomes too volatile.

PEACE-BREAKER SUBSTITUTION

It's impossible to keep the peace if you don't know how to find replacement behaviors for the old negative behaviors. When you notice behaviors that cause conflict, substitute them with behaviors that promote calm and connection.

Step 1: Circle the Peace-Breakers You Recognize in Yourself
Interrupting or talking over someone.

- Sarcasm or dismissive comments.
- Blaming instead of expressing feelings.
- Raising your voice or yelling.
- Bringing up the past in a new argument.
- Avoiding the conversation (stonewalling).

Step 2: Use the Substitution Chart When you notice a peace-breaker in yourself, try using one of these substitute behaviors below to help keep the conversation calm and connected.

PEACE-BREAKER	TRY THIS INSTEAD
Interrupting or talking over	Pause. Let the other person finish. Jot down your thoughts if you're afraid you'll forget.
Sarcasm or dismissive	Speak directly: "I feel hurt when…" or "I need…"
Blaming	Use "I" statements: "I feel…" instead of "You always…"
Raising your voice	Lower your tone and volume, calm voices calm situations.
Bringing up the past	Stay present: focus on the current issue only.
Avoiding the conversation	Say: "I need a break. Let's come back in 20 minutes."

JOURNAL PROMPTS: PAUSE FOR PEACE

1. Do you think you fight too much with your mother/daughter? Explain why you think you are fighting? What do you accomplish?

2. Do you constantly fight about incidents from the past? Why can't you let them go? What do you gain by revisiting the issues?

3. Would you rather win every argument than have peace? Why? Explain the need to win and to be right all the time.

4. Do you think you can pause and listen to another point of view to ease your conflict? How will you do that?

5. Do you know what you want from your mother/daughter? Explain.

6. What techniques from this chapter might work for your mom daughter?

CHAPTER 21
BREAKING UP & RESOURCES FOR EXTREME SITUATIONS

Reading Assignment: Chapter 17 of *The Mother Daughter Relationship Makeover* page 247

We're not going to mince words here, we broke up and went no contact for four years. Our mother-daughter relationship had become so toxic that we were doing more damage to each other than good. We had lost our way and the fighting habit had made it impossible for us to engage in healthy ways with each other. Leslie was fed up and frustrated. Lindsey was enraged, and made the break. It was devastating for both of us. For a mom to lose a child this way is like a knife in the heart even when the child is difficult and even painful to be with. For a mom who shared a business with her daughter, it was even worse.

GHOSTING IS NOT A GOOD MODEL FOR SEPARATION

We needed to separate, but ghosting is probably never a good way to do it. Our story included alcoholism, addiction and mental health struggles–serious issues that needed to be dealt with in therapy and recovery groups. The dysfunctional family model had done its damage for generations, and we both had to find new ways to be with each other if we could be in each other's lives happily. We were also fighting about money and responsibility.

The escalation of problems, like communication, misunderstandings, and chronic anger are not uncommon in dysfunctional families. You get stuck in your own point of view and can't find a path to relationship healing. Now, we like to think, had someone handed this book to us then, we would have had a solutions guide for relationship healing. Did we have to break all contact to work on ourselves? It's a really good question. How toxic were we? How determined were we to vanquish our "enemy?"

It's hard to remember now. We did need to get away from each other and do some solo growing up. Yes, even moms need to grow up.

As you consider whether breaking up is necessary, we ask you, how toxic are you? Has your relationship become one of complete misery? Do you find any joy or comfort with your mother/daughter, or are there issues so serious that being in each other's lives is detrimental?

Knowing when it is time for a break in a relationship is a challenge. But at some point, it may be the healthiest option. We do want to encourage you to be honest about things you may find annoying or issues that are truly toxic and destructive.

EXAMPLES OF TOXIC BEHAVIOR

Chronic emotional or verbal abuse - this can include constantly criticizing or belittling your choices, gaslighting your reality, or making fun of you.

Untreated alcoholism or addiction - we know it well and will be the first to say if someone is putting the family or others at risk with their refusal to treat their addiction or alcoholism you have the right to cut contact and ask them not to be in your space. If you are under 18 and this is your mom, we have some resources listed in the last section.

Untreated mental illness - this can be hard to recognize when you're growing up if no one talks about it or others are making excuses. If your mom or daughter exhibits paranoia, delusions, severe mood swings, you've become her caregiver or scapegoat, or you have to walk on eggshells to avoid her emotional outbursts, you are living with someone who has untreated mental health issues.

Consistent financial sabotage or exploitation - a mom or daughter who throws the family into financial chaos for whatever reasons is going to do a lot of harm. From gambling, to compulsive spending, to taking credit cards out in other family members' names, financial destruction is cause for separation.

Physical or sexual abuse - this should go without saying but here's your permission to never speak to a mother or daughter who beat you or sexually abused you. This behavior is the opposite of what a mother should do and while you may want to forgive her at some point, a dangerous person is a dangerous person, even when you're related to them.

SIGNS YOU NEED A BREAK

If you're still wondering how bad your situation is then consider these signs and mark down how many you experience.

- Every conversation ends badly.
- You feel terrible about yourself after seeing her or speaking to her.
- She exhausts you at every opportunity.
- She won't respect your boundaries.
- She won't respect you.
- You're in therapy working on yourself, and she simply won't take any responsibility for her part.
- You feel guilty for not wanting contact but worse after seeing her.

EMOTIONAL IMPACT OF TOXIC BEHAVIOR

While we know it's not easy to separate, we want to remind you of what the results of a toxic relationship with a mom (or daughter) can be if left untreated:

- Chronic self-doubt and low self-worth.
- Depression and anxiety.
- Emotional dysregulation.
- Fear of abandonment.
- Attracting controlling or dominant partners.
- People-pleasing.
- Dissociation or numbing.

FEAR OF BREAKING UP

Since we've been through this, we know the worries. What will happen to my mom/daughter if I leave? Will she be OK? If there are any financial or family strings, what will happen there? Whose side will people take? Who will people believe? Will I be OK on my own? These are all valid questions. But, you don't have to answer them right now. The answer to these questions is to let them go. You can't control how other people will behave, but you have to save yourself. Here's the truth, none of this is fatal. You can get through all of this and heal your heart and soul no matter what has happened. It starts with ending the drama and giving yourself the quiet and space and time you need to do whatever work will help you understand and heal from what's happened.

ROADMAP TO SEPARATION

This is an agonizing moment, but you're here and you're ready so these are steps you can follow:

1. What kind of separation do you want?

A. No contact - total separation.
B. Limited contact - structured, short calls or visits.
C. Time-limited break - let's not speak for weeks, months, and reevaluate.

2. Prepare for grief and pushback - this goes against nature and doesn't feel good at first.

A. Have a plan for your sadness if you need one (therapist, friend, support group).
B. Be prepared for rage, tantrums, whatever resistance she puts up.

3. **Explain what's happening.**
   A. Communicate what your plan is clearly and without emotion.
   B. Use whatever form of communication is safe - call, text, email.
   C. Avoid any dramatic confrontation.

4. **Protect your peace.**
   A. She won't stop sending you rageful emails. Block her.
   B. Social media posts hurting your soul - unfriend, hide, mute.
   C. Family making you feel bad? Ask them not to mention her for a while.

ADD TO YOUR DICTIONARY
Active Listening
Healthy Communication
De-escalation Tools
Emotional dysregulation
Toxic behavior
Dissociation

JOURNAL PROMPTS: EXTREME SITUATIONS

1. Have you identified any toxic behaviors in your relationship with your mom/daughter? What are they? Explain and describe the issues.

2. Have you tried any conflict resolution tools that have failed? What were they? Why did they not succeed?

3. Did you recognize any serious signs to consider? Which ones?

4. Do you have an effective support system? Who is in it?

5. Do you think you should talk to a professional or learn more about separation when necessary? Please explain.

6. Make a pros and cons list about the relationship now.

"MY STORY"

You are at a significant point in your mother/daughter relationship. You have gained new insights and knowledge about the dynamics of the mother/daughter relationship through your readings and learning activities.

Take some time to read back through your journal. Make notes and look for connections and intersections.

What is your gut telling you? How do you plan on proceeding? Thoughtfully consider the implications of this decision for both sides of the mother/daughter relationship.

"LETTING GO MEANS TO COME TO THE REALIZATION THAT SOME PEOPLE ARE PART OF YOUR HISTORY, BUT NOT A PART OF YOUR DESTINY."

– STEVE MARABOLI

CHAPTER 22
STEP 4: HEALING & RECONCILIATION

Reading Assignment: Chapter 18 of *The Mother Daughter Relationship Makeover* page 263

ACCEPTING YOUR PART

Remember above where we said this is where the rubber meets the road? It's right here. Don't get us wrong, these are complicated dynamics. This is when you feel utterly hurt by your mom or daughter, and the last thing you want to do is to look at where you were at fault. Maybe you weren't at fault, maybe the harms were done to you, but this work can still be valuable in terms of how you carry what happened with you into the future.

See, we know from our own experience that the only way you can understand what exactly happened in your history with your mom or daughter is to do some inventory work. Inventory work allows you to use examples of what's happened to see where your accountability lies.

The issue is not all family members are going to be able to take accountability. Not all family members can say they are sorry. Some mothers and daughters will only be able to find blame with you and never see their part. That's why you need some clear information on what happened so you can say sorry for what was on you and let the rest go. If someone else can't, that's their problem.

ACCEPTANCE IS CRUCIAL

Accepting your part—whether in a conflict, a mistake, or a life situation—puts you in control of your own growth. If you don't own your role, you stay stuck in a cycle of blame, resentment, or denial, which blocks progress. Do you know someone who has no self-awareness? Do they drive you crazy with their judgment of other people when they often have the very same traits they criticize? Don't be one of those people. Learn to understand where your behavior hurts other people and taking responsibility for it is the most powerful thing you can do for yourself.

For us accepting that we each played a part in causing pain was the turning point. Our relationship became more about getting along than winning points and trying to control each other's behavior.

We strongly advise you to ask someone for help with this part of the recovery process. While we provide you with tools to start this process a sponsor, therapist, or counselor or counselor can help you to accept two points of view.

INVENTORY

Please begin on page 265 of *The Mother Daughter Relationship Makeover* with the resentment inventory and read through for the explanation. Complete your resentment inventory and then continue with the fear and anxiety, and harmful behaviors inventories. After you thoughtfully complete each one, pause for a moment. Take a break and then return to them. Add or change anything that needs additional thought.

QUICK INVENTORY EXAMPLES

Resentment Examples

- I'm mad at my mom because she smokes too much.
- I'm mad at my daughter because she demands I care for her children.

Fear and Anger Inventory

- I'm fearful that if my mom doesn't take better care of herself, she will get sick.
- I'm fearful that if my daughter doesn't become a responsible parent, something bad will happen.

Harmful Behaviors Inventory

- I can now see that my behavior feels controlling to my mom, and she has the right to manage her health the way she wants.
- I can now see how nagging my daughter about her parenting and my time is fruitless. I need boundaries for myself.

STAY POSITIVE

Don't forget to reflect and list the positives when you do this work. If your mom constantly nags you about healthcare but you know it's because she's worried and she cares, remember to add that your mom cares about you. That she spends time wondering if you're keeping up with your care. The same goes for moms–if your daughter drives you crazy about something but you know behind the actions are love or concern, that deserves recognition. What is underneath the behavior, caring and concern or criticism and judgment? It's important to know the difference.

A favorite quote of ours is, "When you change the way you look at things, the things you look at change." by Max Plank. Think about that. When you shift your thinking and look at events from a unique perspective, keep an open mindset, and do the work, you are moving towards recovery.

MINDSET AND PERSPECTIVE

Mindset and perspective shape how we perceive, communicate, and respond to each other. Our mindset is going to determine our emotional response, and our perspective will shape how we understand each other. This means, if we are stuck in patterns and beliefs that are no longer serving us and our relationship, we need to change them.

For example, Lindsey stopped thinking Leslie was the most controlling person on earth. She began to understand that mom's habit of watching Lindsey's food habits and moods was based in fear for her health. Lindsey stopped reacting to casual comments and began to view her mother in a more loving way.

When Leslie understood how anxious and sensitive Lindsey was, she was able to give Lindsey more grace to be uncomfortable at times and not have to make everything right for her. Moms don't have to fix everything. Lindsey was entitled to have anxiety without Leslie interfering.

PRACTICE MINDSET SHIFTS & PERSPECTIVE BUILDING

- Talk to different people for a new point of view.
- Practice empathy by putting yourself in your mother or daughter's shoes.
- Assume the positive instead of the negative.
- Read, Pray, and Meditate on the thoughts you are trying to change.
- Learn about Positive Psychology and techniques to employ it.
- Let go of the need to "win."
- Find some humor in your differences.
- Always pause before reacting and consider all sides.

"THE PRACTICE OF FORGIVENESS IS OUR MOST IMPORTANT CONTRIBUTION TO THE HEALING OF THE WORLD."

- MARIANNE WILLIASON

LEARNING ACTIVITIES

FINDING PATTERNS

Using all of the information in the personal inventories you did above, use some different colored highlighters and code your inventories. Look for patterns that keep recurring. If you need examples, they are provided on pages 267 – 268.

Take your time with this process. What are you discovering? Follow the process beginning on page 268 to deeply reflect on what you are discovering. Be honest. What is preventing you from being the best version of yourself? This is transformational work if you trust the process and do it with an open mind.

"MY STORY"
Add your key aha's you discovered from the personal inventories work.

ADD TO YOUR DICTIONARY

Acceptance

Accountability

CHAPTER 23
FORGIVENESS & HEALING

Reading Assignment: Chapter 19 of *The Mother Daughter Relationship Makeover* page 281

Are you someone who is good at forgiving others or do you hold a grudge? Here's a fact, forgiveness is an action or idea that you may need to take again and again. Sometimes we have to keep re-forgiving someone. But, forgiveness is an essential step in the healing and recovery process.

Forgiveness is defined as a conscious, deliberate decision to release feelings of resentment toward someone who has harmed you.

While releasing resentment is healthy, there's more to forgiveness than just letting go of the anger. For example: forgiveness does not include forgetting what was done. Forgiveness is not condoning the harm someone has done to you. And forgiveness doesn't mean you have to see the person again or reconcile. Forgiveness is entirely for your health and wellbeing.

Forgiveness allows you to move towards healing. Anger, hatred, and resentments take a huge toll on your health. Holding on to these emotions for decades wreaks havoc with your mind and body.

Forgiveness is a choice, and you can learn how to forgive. Think about forgiveness as a gift to yourself, not to someone else. The purpose is to bring you peace, closure, and hope.

Forgiveness is a process that takes time and energy. Now healing is another matter altogether.

Healing in a relationship is the process of repairing emotional wounds, rebuilding trust, and creating a healthier dynamic between two people.

Healing is not about erasing the past, but rather learning how to move forward with greater understanding, empathy, and growth. We've discussed some of the important reasons healing is so crucial; and those include, improving future relationships, healing your old wounds, and learning to turn a negative past into a positive future.

It's impossible to reconcile safely and happily without some healing, so we'll be clear in saying please work on yourself and understand what happened with your mother or daughter if you do want to reconcile. We know from experience there has to be some space and lessening of emotions when returning to this relationship, so we have some ideas to help you on your journey of forgiveness and healing.

A FEW COMPELLING REASONS FOR FORGIVENESS

1. It improves our physical health. The stress we have imposed on our bodies eases. Our immune systems respond and recover when we forgive.

2. Forgiveness improves our mental health. Depression and anxiety are reduced and hope increases.

3. Forgiveness can make us feel happier. Letting go of past resentments creates spaces for more positive thinking.

HOW TO GET IN THE FORGIVING MINDSET

As we shared above, forgiveness takes practice and not everyone knows where to start so we put together a forgiveness path for you.

1. Acknowledge the hurt - sometimes we've held it in so long we forget to let it out.

2. Write it down - get clear on what needs to be forgiven.

3. Make a choice that you are going to work on forgiving.

4. Work on changing your perspective about what happened by reading books on forgiveness, listening to podcasts or speakers on forgiveness and do some work on what forgiving is going to look like for you.

5. Pray, meditate, and open your mind to feeling different.

6. If you are struggling to forgive, seek support from a professional or support group.

7. Give time time - it takes time to change your mind so give yourself grace on the trip.

9. Check in with yourself after a few weeks to see if there's change and dig deeper if need be.

A FEW COMPELLING REASONS FOR HEALING

1. Frees you from your past. Holding onto pain and resentment is a curse. Being on the other side of resentment ourselves, we can promise letting go of hurts from the past makes life worth living.

2. Improves self-esteem. Not kidding here. Healing the mommy issues will do more for your self-esteem than you can imagine.

3. Protects your mental and emotional health. When we roam the world unhealed we see it through a negative lens and people see us through a negative lens.

4. Restores self-worth, and isn't that what all of this is about?

5. Increases inner peace. We all need more of that no matter who you are and what's happened in your life.

EXAMPLES:

Marie was furious at her daughter for years because her daughter demanded she help with her kids and expected lots of time and attention. Her daughter took advantage of her, treated her badly, and never even considered repaying her for the money she had spent on the grandkids. The resentment, which turned into true rage actually caused her terrible rosacea to return. Marie was sick and miserable for months. It wasn't until her friend suggested she do some therapy and grief work around her daughter that the rosacea actually subsided and the medication began to work again. Don't think ongoing anger and resentment don't lead to real physical manifestations because they absolutely do.

Amanda was angry at her mom for her overspending. Amanda helps fund her mother's life, and has always been happy to help because she does well financially. But her mother took advantage and spent it like it's going out of style. Amanda became so obsessed with watching the Amazon account, the PayPal, the credit cards, and cash sitting around in her mom's house that it made her paranoid. She spent less time on work and family and more time brooding. Her suffering mental health around her mother had real consequences on her own life and relationships. On the advice of her husband, Amanda got some much needed therapy and learned how to limit the amount of financial support she offered, telling her mom she simply couldn't afford it. This made her mom have to take responsibility for her own spending. If mom is not responsible, then other methods of control can be put in place.

HOW TO GET INTO HEALING

Getting into the healing mindset is a journey that requires intentionality, self-awareness, and patience. It's not about "getting over" things, but rather about working through them in a way that brings peace, growth, and freedom. No one likes to be told what to do or how to be emotionally healthy. We all have to come to healing practices our own way. So be patient with yourself and your mom/daughter if she's slow to change.

HERE'S HOW YOU CAN START:

1. Feel your feelings. Sit in the discomfort and sadness but the only way forward is through, so if the tears need to flow let them.

2. You're a volunteer not a victim. The minute you decide you're not a victim, you're not. Letting go of the victim mentality is critical to healing.

3. Forgive yourself (and your mom/daughter) for whatever happened and whatever you and she needed to do to get through it. It's over and you did the best you could with the information you had at the time.

4. Decide if you need professional help or support groups for guidance. If you have experienced trauma or abuse at the hands of your mom/daughter, professional help is advised. We did it, and it made all the difference.

5. Take care of your body with self-care, exercise, and nourishment. This is the time to raise your endorphins and feel good naturally with anything you can do to care for your physical self.

6. Take care of your mental health with exercise, meditation, reading or recovery work, listen to uplifting or self-help podcasts, shows, etc. Make no mistake, this is work and it requires homework. You will see progress in this work we swear.

7. Develop a spiritual life. If you have religion or spirituality, great. Lean into it for comfort and understanding. If you don't, now is a good time to explore what spiritual practices might give you comfort.

8. Help others and animals. It will make you and them feel better.

LEARNING ACTIVITIES

DEVELOPING A FORGIVENESS PLAN

Forgiveness is a process that takes time. It won't happen in a day or even a week. For forgiveness to work, you need to create a plan that includes accountability. In your journal, develop your plan. Include these items:

- Clearly state what needs to be forgiven. Include the details.
- Select the tools from Chapter 19 that you are willing to experiment with. Make a list of them in your journal or calendar them into your day for a couple of weeks. If necessary, get a buddy, relative or friend to help keep you accountable.

- Ask for help. If you are not working with a mental health professional, reach out to a faith-based support group or a close friend or mentor.

- Share your need for forgiveness and your action plan with them. Ask the support person or group to set a schedule with you for checking in. (If you are not in a position to reach out, ignore this piece).

- Journal about each step in your forgiveness process. What is working? What is not? What can you try next?

MY ACTION PLAN

1. What from our list of tools will you try?
   _____
   _____
   _____
   _____

2. Can you make a schedule you will stick to?
   _____
   _____
   _____
   _____

3. How can you hold yourself accountable for keeping that schedule?
   _____
   _____
   _____
   _____

JOURNAL PROMPTS: FORGIVENESS

1. How do you feel about forgiveness? Do you forgive easily? Does your family have feelings about forgiveness? What are they?

2. Have you been forgiving toward your mother/daughter? Has she been forgiving toward you? Explain

3. Do any of the tools for forgiveness appeal to you? What might you try from the list? Can you schedule it into your life?

4. Have you ever thought about healing before?

5. Do you think you or your mother/daughter need healing?

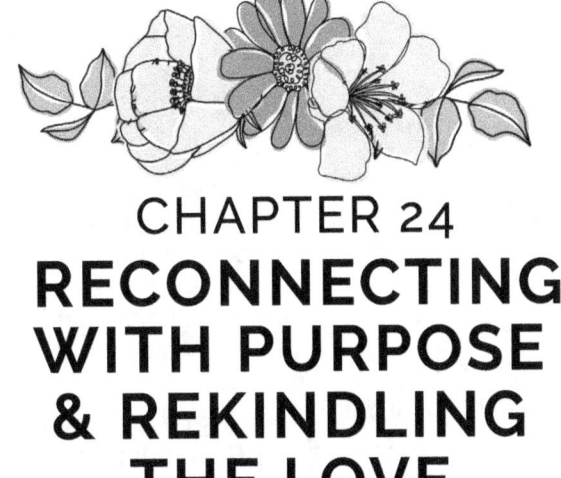

CHAPTER 24
RECONNECTING WITH PURPOSE & REKINDLING THE LOVE

Reading Assignment: Chapter 20 of *The Mother Daughter Relationship Makeover* page 293

Reconnecting with purpose, and rekindling the love is going to look different for everyone and might take longer for some than others. There is no straight line with this type of relationship recovery and there will be ups and downs. Don't be disappointed if this step does not happen on the timeline you initially think or want. Leslie was not ready to reconcile with Lindsey when Lindsey was ready. We tiptoed in with emails and calls for a while. But, if you're here, reconciliation is on your mind or a possibility for the future. Let's unpack it with purpose.

While you have done a great deal of work to get here and you must be a seeker of truth and healing, this is not a Disney or Hallmark movie. This is reality and given what has happened in your relationship, now is the time to decide what comes next. What kind of relationship do you feel is the best for your mental, physical, and spiritual health? You should start this new chapter with your mother or daughter setting all the new standards you want for each other. The question is, how do you get there? And, remember, this should look very different because you have done the painstaking work of exploring the causes of the challenges in your relationship. Let's start with what you want based on what you now know.

WHAT KIND OF RELATIONSHIP DO YOU WANT

This may be a gut-check moment for many women. Maybe you don't like what you discovered here, and it's best for your emotional and physical health to have a limited relationship with your mother or daughter. If that is the case, we're proud of you for making that decision. We were there once. It does not mean it will be this way forever. You can create a new format for your relationship. But be honest, and don't ghost your mother or daughter without warning.

Deciding what kind of relationship to have with your mom/daughter depends on your history together, your emotional needs, and what's possible given both of your willingness to engage. It's important to be realistic about her capacity to meet you where you are and to set boundaries that protect your peace.

HOW TO DECIDE WHAT RELATIONSHIP TO HAVE WITH YOUR MOM:

Assess the Current Relationship
- Is our relationship healthy or toxic?
- Do I feel safe being myself around her?
- Is there mutual respect, or is it one-sided?
- What do I want to keep, change, or let go of?

Identify Your Needs & Boundaries
- Do I need more emotional distance?
- Do I want a deeper connection?
- What boundaries would make me feel safer?
- Am I willing to do the work to improve things?

Consider Her Capacity for Change
- Is she self-aware and open to growth?
- Has she shown willingness to respect boundaries?
- Is she emotionally safe to be around?

You can want a certain relationship, but if she isn't capable of meeting you there, **accepting reality** is key.

TYPES OF MOTHER-DAUGHTER RELATIONSHIPS

Close & Nurturing
- Mutual respect, emotional safety, and supportive.
- Open, honest conversations with healthy boundaries.
- Feels like a safe space, full of love and understanding.
- This kind of relationship works best for moms who are emotionally available, loving, and willing to work on the relationship.

Work in Progress
- Some emotional connection, but issues to work through.
- Both are willing to heal past wounds and improve communication.
- Requires effort, therapy, or intentional rebuilding.
- This kind of relationship works best for moms who may have hurt you but are open to change.

Surface-Level/Polite Relationship
- Basic communication, but limited emotional depth.
- Avoids deep topics to prevent conflict.
- Keep things light to maintain peace.
- This kind of relationship works best for moms who are difficult but still important in your life.

Low Contact
- Limited interaction to protect your emotional well-being.
- Boundaries around when/how you communicate.
- Focuses on what's necessary (holidays, major events). This kind of relationship works best for moms who are toxic, manipulative, or emotionally unsafe.

No Contact
- Cutting ties completely for self-preservation.
- Removing yourself from an unhealthy dynamic.
- Choosing peace over a painful, unchangeable relationship.
- This kind of relationship works best for moms who are abusive, narcissistic, or unwilling to respect boundaries.

MOVING FORWARD

Our hope is that through this process you will be ready to start over with some new and improved techniques to get along better.

As you think about what a new relationship can be, read *the five characteristics of healthy relationships beginning on page 299*. Rate yourself on each of them. A five means you can do this, three means maybe, and one means I really need help with this one. Are you willing to work on your low characteristic grades to improve yourself and your relationship? Remember, recovery is a process.

FIVE CHARACTERISTICS OF HEALTHY RELATIONSHIPS

Master the five characteristics of healthy relationships and we guarantee your life will be improved. *Please see page 299 of the book* for the full descriptions.

- Honest Communication and Respect
- Acceptance of Each Other
- Having Love and Compassion
- Involvement and Collaboration
- Healthy Coping Skills

Make an assessment/rate chart. Ask yourself after doing this assessment if you feel you are ready to rekindle in a warm and loving way? There is no judgment or wrong or right with any of this, only is this the right thing to do right now.

Characteristics of Healthy Relationships Assessment Chart Rate and Comment On The Work You Need To Do

AREA	HEALTHY RELATIONSHIP ASSESSMENT
Honest Communication and Respect	
Acceptance of Each Other	
Having Love and Compassion	
Involvement and Collaboration	
Healthy Coping Skills	

REKINDLING THE LOVE

Maybe one of the things you've learned on this journey is that you truly want to have a loving relationship with your mom or daughter. You know what? There's nothing wrong or abnormal about that! It's a great outcome to have. The important question for this piece of the puzzle is what are you willing to give up to make that healthy, loving relationship happen? Because the exact relationship you want may not be possible.

You may have to behave in new or uncomfortable ways to make your mom or daughter feel safe. But, trust us, if there is some kind of safe relationship to be had with your mom or daughter, it is usually worth it. Feeling safe means your mom/daughter won't criticize every time she opens her mouth. Feeling safe means your mom/daughter won't ask for or demand things that you don't want to give. Feeling safe means kindness is always the impulse in every response. This may be new to you. Safety is feeling appreciated, accepted, and well...safe.

WHAT KIND OF RELATIONSHIP DO YOU WANT

- Daily Interactions
- Weekly Phone Or Video Calls
- Monthly Check-ins
- Peaceful Holiday Reunions
- Yearly Recognition

SAFE ACTIVITIES TO SHARE

Now that you are considering what kind of relationship you want to have, bring in whatever activities or communications that will work. If you decide you want regular interactions, what do you both like to do or what are you willing to do? For example, maybe your mom or daughter loves to hike with the dog or spend hours shopping for food and then cooking a meal. Would you be willing to do those things with her even if they are not your favorite? Making someone feel safe and supported sometimes means inconveniencing yourself a little.

If you're only ready for calls or holidays and want to ensure those go smoothly, what are the non-triggering topics for you to talk about? How can you prepare yourself to stay calm if the conversation or event starts to go sideways? Having a plan, clear boundaries, and a tool kit for newer healthier behaviors is part of the job of rekindling.

Don't forget to bring back anything you loved to do together in the past. Lindsey and Leslie returned to old happy habits when they rekindled. They crafted chocolates and baked together, walked with the dogs, visited old favorite places and restaurants–anything to promote good memories to add to the old ones. Every mom and daughter has a few good memories of old times. Bring them out and show how they are cherished.

JOURNAL PROMPTS: RECONNECTING WITH PURPOSE

1. What kind of relationship do you want to have?

2. What do you want your interactions to be like?

3. Are there any gestures that would be meaningful to your mother/daughter?

4. Are you someone who brings up the past a lot? Why? What do I get from doing it?

5. If so, do you think you could practice letting that go? Why or why not?

6. What might be some good activities that you can do together that will rebuild your relationship?

"MY STORY"

My Reconnection Plan. It is time for you to envision what your new mother-daughter relationship looks like. Respond to the journal prompts *(page 304)* to assist you in creating your plan.

CHAPTER 25
THE RECOVERY LIFESTYLE COPING & RESOURCES FOR THIS PROCESS

Reading Assignment: Chapter 21 of *The Mother Daughter Relationship Makeover* page 305

Congratulations for getting to this milestone. Self-discovery is a challenging task. As we end this book, we know that we, as a mother and daughter, love each other and want to be connected. We also have learned the importance of our own worth, our own dreams, and nurturing our own lives independently of each other. Having strong lives that are independent of each other helps us support each other without losing ourselves.

BOOK REVIEW

Read about Lindsey's recovery lifestyle that began with sobriety and evolved into so much more. Then, consider Leslie's pathway to healing and recovery. Each found her own coping methods, healing tools and ways to find joy in life. We'll add Lindsey's here.

LINDSEY'S RECOVERY LIFESTYLE

I developed what I call "the recovery lifestyle," during my own long road from getting sober, to learning an entirely new way of living, to healing, going through therapy and different avenues of recovery, and finally as I built a career and focused on reaching my potential and achieving goals. There are five parts to this "recovery lifestyle" of mine and they include: spirituality, nutrition, fitness, advocacy, and self-help.

Spirituality is important because, whether you believe in God or not, it addresses fundamental human needs and can provide meaning, direction, and community–especially in times of struggle. Spirituality is valuable for mothers and daughters trying to find meaning in what happened between them because it fosters hope, compassion, and inner peace.

If you struggle to find meaning, spiritual practices like meditation or personal practices of self-reflection can create incredible relief. Seeking a spiritual mentor or community is also fabulous for some people who need a fresh perspective and positivity. I became a Nichiren Buddhist in recovery and the chanting has helped with anxiety and mindfulness, and the community has been another saving grace in knowing like-minded people who care about the same things I do.

SPIRITUALITY CHECK

1. Do you have a spiritual or religious practice? If not, is there one you'd be interested in learning more about?

2. Would you consider trying any practices or new-age spirituality like: Yoga, meditation, sound baths, breathwork, nature-walks, energy work like Reiki, or therapeutic art or music classes?

3. Would you commit to 30 days of gratitude lists? Every day you write a list of ten things you are grateful for like: Today, I am grateful for my dog, dance, music, coffee, the ocean, my friends, funny books, etc.

NUTRITION

Nutrition makes an incredible difference to your health when you are paying attention to it. But, making the change to a healthy diet can be a daunting and a life-long challenge. We love sweets, potatoes, pasta, chips, bread (especially if it's fried), and anything fried.

It's taken decades to give up those habits of containers of greasy Chinese food, slathered pork BBQ, and extra fries but when we did, here's what happened... The weight dropped off, skin cleared up, energy increased, and with time, we lost the taste for these things. That doesn't mean we don't have occasional days when we indulge in foods we used to love. We just don't have the fatty, salty, crunchy, sugary cravings every day and have to battle through them. You can get used to eating healthier foods.

NUTRITION CHECK:

1. What's your food look like? Are you a healthy eater, unhealthy eater, you can do what you want and moderate, or is food both your best friend and worst enemy. Take it from a former over and under eater - I know what it's like to love and hate food. Take a few moments to write about your current diet.

2. Do you want to make changes to your diet? Can you add nutrition that will help with whatever ails you? Take a moment to journal about what your ideal diet would look like. Also write for a moment on whether you know what would improve your diet, like have you done the research? For example, I try to eat as much Turmeric as possible because it helps with inflammation.

3. For people who want to improve their diet or nutrition, would you be willing to try something different for 30 days?

TIPS TO IMPROVE YOUR NUTRITION/DIET:

- Get professional help, there's lots online for free.
- Try meal kits.
- Plan your meals and snacks ahead. That way you're in control.
- Eat enough protein in every meal.
- Learn to read labels to limit salt, fat, and sugar.
- Listen to your body. Don't eat when you're not hungry.
- Cut out or cut down the sugar!
- Portion size matters. Use smaller plates.
- Eat as many whole foods as possible.

MOVE YOUR BODY

I used to call this section exercise but it's not just about exercise. Moving your body in any way is really what I'm talking about. A body that doesn't move will stagnate, become weaker, lose muscle and mobility. If you don't move, there will come a time when you can't move. A body that moves will find joy along the way. So, whether you're a walker, a Yogi, a lover of Tai Chi, or learning how to pole dance is your activity of choice, great. All that I care about is that you are moving your body enough to keep it young and limber, and that you break enough of a sweat to release Endorphins, the feel-good chemical.

Moving your body is tied in the top three for me because it is a triple-threat. If you are engaging in regular movement or exercise, it helps your mental health by boosting those endorphins we were talking about, which also means you feel less anxious and less depressed. Every single mental health professional who has treated me has encouraged me to exercise, particularly during stressful times, and it always helps.

In addition to physical benefits, exercise can provide community. I've joined gyms, yoga studios, cycling studios, and more; and every time I'm delighted by the community that comes with it. We also have regular dog walking meet-ups in the morning. That works, too. When I was sad and alone during holidays, I went to exercise classes and felt better. At times when I was anxious and depressed, I focused on my physical health and body; and it gave me purpose. And, finally, if you're a little vain like me, exercise can help keep you in shape. It's a way to improve your body and health with work and positive discipline as opposed to unhealthy diets or restricting food. Like I said, kill three birds with one exercise class.

EXERCISE CHECK:

1. Do you enjoy any kind of exercise or moving your body? Why or why not?

2. Do you think you could benefit from more physical activity, a new community of people, or stronger focus and discipline on your physical health?

3. What would you be willing to commit to for 30 days to make small improvements?

TIPS TO BRING MOVEMENT INTO YOUR LIFE PERMANENTLY

- Daily Walks or Runs with or without a dog.
- 30-Day Fitness Challenges. Find these everywhere online - Google, Pinterest, Youtube.
- Workout Apps or Online Classes. These changed my life during the pandemic, and I still use them.
- Outdoor Adventures. Get some nature while you move! Water sports, Hiking, Biking.
- Dance It Out. This you can do at home, with online incentives, or try ballroom.
- Strength Training. Okay, you may need a gym for weight training if that's your thing.
- Yoga, Pilates, Sculpt, Barre, HIIT or any class that moves you.
- Sports or Recreational Activities, again this can be in nature.
- Mini Workouts. We do this all day. A few wall exercises are like a facelift for your body.
- Reward Yourself. What is your reward? A massage, a long soak in the tub? A piece of dark chocolate. If you move, that's a reward in itself, but think of something you love and gift yourself.

SELF-IMPROVEMENT/SELF-HELP

You wouldn't be here, reading this book, or at the end of this workbook if you didn't believe in self-help and self-improvement. Like everything in this world, self-help is what you make of it. If you take the time to learn, become self-aware, practice new behaviors and new coping skills, it works. If you half-measure it, it doesn't.

I am a great lover and appreciator of self-help because it has radically changed my life. Recovery programs, rehabs, and sponsors taught me how to be sober, and that was a miracle. They taught me how to live life without drugs and alcohol, how to feel my feelings, be accountable for my behavior, and even how to be of service in this world. Life-changing.

1. Professional Help: You can get professional help in many ways. Coaching with a certified life coach, counseling or therapy with a social worker or clinical psychologist. 12 step groups or group therapy in the area you choose. Online therapy can be very helpful, too.. Do some research about what kind of professional help will work best for you, and be sure that you check references before working with anyone. Also, if you choose a group and don't like the members, move on to a different one. We offer some resources below.

2. Books: We love to read, and we guess you do, too. Browse in your library, on Amazon or your local book store. Self help is everywhere. Once again, not everyone will have the same values or goals as you.

3. Self-Reflection and Mindset tools: Here's where journaling and daily gratitude journals can keep you in a positive frame of mind. Affirmations, whether from an app or a book or your inner circle or religion also provide the daily reminders everyone needs to feel okay even when things seem to be falling apart around you. The only constant is change, so remember that you have power over your attitude and that can change your life.

4. Learning and Skill Development: Want to learn something new? Take a class. Go online and explore all the things you can do to improve your life even if you can't leave your zip code.

5. Positive Psychology: This is a shift from studying mental illness and what's wrong with your life to focusing on wellness and what makes you happy and satisfied. Positive psychology helps people find meaning and create a more fulfilling life. This is another aspect of mindset and perspective that we've talked about before. Changing perspective provides the foundation for taking action.

SELF-IMPROVEMENT CHECK:

1. Are there any areas you want to work on? What are they?

2. What kind of work would you be willing to do to see improvement?

3. What's one book or app or activity you want to try for self-improvement?

ADVOCACY

One of the throughlines of my life in recovery has been service. Service to other people, service to animals, service to the elderly, whoever needs help, I'll help. Want to know why? It's without a doubt, the time that I feel the best about myself. I feel whole and satisfied when I help other people or advocate for a cause I care about. I have the good fortune of having service in my family for generations, so it comes easy to me, but I carry it on today in lots of new ways too.

When I was going through the separation with my mom, it helped to have a place to put my love and caring. I've helped collect and deliver food for people in need, collected school supplies for kids, cleaned up the beach, you get the idea. There are tons of things you can do to be of service that have nothing to do with giving money.

You can donate your time and skills, you can become a part of a community working to make something better, and I absolutely promise it will make you feel better. For me, it's easy. Recovery and mental health are big causes for me, but I also support many causes for humans and animals. Now's the time to think about what you care about or what skills or time you can use to help others.

ADVOCACY CHECK:

1. Is there any cause you could get behind? If not, is there anything you might get more involved with from church activities to tutoring children or teens? Community gardening, helping with a food bank. Reading to animals in a shelter. There are literally thousands of ways to be a helper and improve your own life.

2. Do you think you would benefit from some kind of community service or advocacy?

"MY STORY"
Your story does not end here. It is time for you to author your new story. Create a vision board with lots of pictures and ideas. Who is the new you? How does a new mother-daughter relationship fit into your vision?

LEARNING ACTIVITIES

WEEKLY RECOVERY PLANNER

Recovery is a journey toward a balanced and fulfilling life. This planner is designed to help you strengthen your body, mind, spirit, and relationships. Each day offers a focus to keep you intentional, motivated, and moving forward with purpose.

Use this schedule on the next page as a flexible guide. Swap days or themes if it suits your week, recovery is about creating a life that works for you.

WEEKLY RECOVERY PLANNER		
SUNDAY	**FOCUS: REFLECTION & RENEWAL** Start your week with clarity and gratitude.	
TASKS: ☐ Review the past week: What worked? What needs adjusting? ☐ Plan the week ahead (meetings, therapy, self-care goals). ☐ Celebrate your wins (days sober, breakthroughs, showing up).		**NOTES:** What do you want to carry into this new week? _____ _____ _____
MONDAY	**FOCUS: EMOTIONAL CHECK-IN** Ground yourself in honesty and self-awareness.	
TASKS: ☐ Attend therapy or counseling. ☐ Practice a coping skill (journaling, grounding, art, meditation). ☐ Connect with a supportive friend, mentor, or sponsor.		**NOTES:** What emotions surfaced today? How did you process them? _____ _____
TUESDAY	**FOCUS: PURPOSE & PASSION** Tap into what makes life meaningful.	
TASKS: ☐ Work on a personal goal or creative project. ☐ Explore your passions (writing, music, service, learning). ☐ Reflect on your "why" for recovery.		**NOTES:** What lit you up today? How did it fuel your recovery? _____ _____
WEDNESDAY	**FOCUS: PHYSICAL HEALTH** Strengthen your body to support your mind.	
TASKS: ☐ Move your body for 30 minutes (walk, yoga, gym). ☐ Prepare nourishing meals or snacks. ☐ Join a support group meeting.		**NOTES:** How did movement or nutrition affect your mood and energy? _____ _____
THURSDAY	**FOCUS: SPIRITUAL GROWTH** Connect with something bigger than yourself.	
TASKS: ☐ Practice meditation, prayer, or quiet reflection. ☐ Spend time in nature. ☐ Read or listen to something spiritually uplifting.		**NOTES:** Did you feel more connected or centered today? _____ _____
FRIDAY	**FOCUS: SOCIAL CONNECTION** Invest in relationships that nurture your recovery.	
TASKS: ☐ Plan a sober activity with a friend (coffee, hike, dinner). ☐ Avoid high-risk situations that threaten your progress. ☐ Journal about your relationships (progress, gratitude).		**NOTES:** Who encouraged you today? How did you show up for others? _____ _____
SATURDAY	**FOCUS: SELF-CARE & SERVICE** Balance rest with giving back.	
TASKS: ☐ Engage in a hobby (gardening, painting, music). ☐ Practice relaxation (bath, massage, mindful walk). ☐ Volunteer, mentor, or support someone else in recovery.		**NOTES:** What restored your energy? How did service impact your day? _____ _____

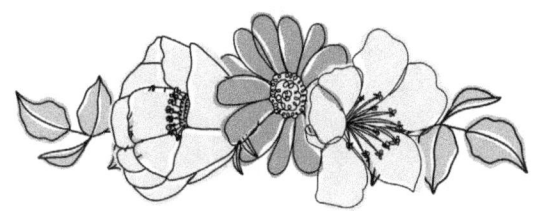

RESOURCES

APPENDIX: RESOURCES FOR LASTING CHANGE

Your journey toward a healthier, more connected mother-daughter relationship doesn't end with these pages. The following books, organizations, and support networks can help you continue growing in understanding, communication, and emotional resilience.

BOOKS ON MOTHER-DAUGHTER RELATIONSHIPS, COMMUNICATION, AND FORGIVENESS

Brené Brown's Atlas of the Heart: Mapping Meaningful Connection and the Language of Human Experience is a great resource to start exploring emotions. "If we want to find the way back to ourselves and one another, we need language and the grounded confidence to both tell our stories and be stewards of the stories that we hear."

The Dance of Connection – Harriet Lerner, Ph.D.
A compassionate guide to speaking honestly and staying connected through conflict.

Mothers Who Can't Love – Susan Forward, Ph.D.
Offers insight and healing strategies for daughters of emotionally unavailable or hurtful mothers.

Will I Ever Be Good Enough? – Karyl McBride, Ph.D.
A path toward self-discovery for daughters of narcissistic mothers.

Radical Forgiveness – Colin Tipping
A fresh framework for moving past resentment and reclaiming inner peace.

Nonviolent Communication – Marshall B. Rosenberg, Ph.D.
A step-by-step approach to expressing needs and listening without judgment.

FAMILY THERAPY & MENTAL HEALTH SUPPORT

Psychology Today Therapist Directory – psychologytoday.com
Find licensed family therapists, counselors, and coaches by location and specialty.

American Association for Marriage and Family Therapy (AAMFT) – aamft.org Locate accredited family therapists trained in communication, boundaries, and conflict resolution.

BetterHelp – betterhelp.com
Online therapy with options for individuals, couples, and families.

National Alliance on Mental Illness (NAMI) Helpline – Call 1-800-950-NAMI or text "Help" to 62640
Free, confidential mental health support, information, and referrals.

FAMILY & SUPPORT GROUPS

Al-Anon Family Groups – al-anon.org
Support for those affected by a loved one's substance abuse, focusing on boundaries and self-care.

Adult Children of Alcoholics/Dysfunctional Families (ACA) – adultchildren.org
Resources and tools for breaking unhealthy family patterns.

Codependents Anonymous (CoDA) – coda.org
Support for building healthier boundaries and self-esteem.

GriefShare – griefshare.org
Group support for navigating loss and life changes.

ONLINE LEARNING & COMMUNICATION SKILLS

The Gottman Institute – gottman.com
Evidence-based tools for building trust, connection, and healthy communication.

TED Talks on Communication & Forgiveness – Search for *Brené Brown (vulnerability), Harriet Lerner (apologies), and Sarah Montana (forgiveness).*

Greater Good Science Center – ggsc.berkeley.edu
Research-based practices for empathy, resilience, and emotional intelligence.

PRAISE

PRAISE FOR THE MOTHER DAUGHTER RELATIONSHIP MAKEOVER: FOUR STEPS TO BRING BACK THE LOVE

"This book is a must for any parent with daughters in their lives. It is like that second parachute you are given, just in case. The book is about understanding, compassion and giving. An emotional road map that is highly recommended even for dads sometimes navigating through tough daughter times." - *The Oshawa/Durham Central Newspaper*

"Unique, effective, exceptionally well organized, thoroughly 'user friendly in presentation, "The Mother-Daughter Relationship Makeover: 4 Steps to Bring Back the Love" is an extraordinary and unreservedly recommended addition to personal reading lists, as well as community and college/university library Self-Help, Parenting, and Mother/Daughter collections and supplemental Parent/Adult Relationship curriculum studies lists." - *The Midwest Book Review, Susan Bethany's Bookshelf*

"A brand-new kind of interactive self-help book that combines actionable information, compelling storytelling, and writing prompts that are guaranteed to bring awareness, understanding, and compassion to mothers and daughters everywhere." - *St. Mary School Newsletter, The Glasgow Missourian*

"Read this book if you and your mother don't get along."
- *Oprah's book club*

"I have never seen a book quite like this. Reading the perspectives of both mother and daughter was a unique experience. When we are 'in it,' it is hard to see past our pain. Leslie and Lindsey widened the lens on mother-daughter relationships so we could see not only the complexity of the problems, but also the journey to repair them. This makeover is a great book on making up with excellent exercises and thought-provoking writing prompts. For best results, I recommend both mother and daughter read it simultaneously and see what happens!" - *Dr. Deborah Sweet, psychologist and trauma specialist*

Goodreads reviews

"My adult daughter and I read this exceptional book together, and it resonated for both of us in so many meaningful ways. We wish that it had been available during the formative years of our mother-daughter relationship. Perhaps our journey toward mutual love and understanding would have been much smoother than it actually was!"

"This book is well-organized and very readable, and it offers practical ideas for repairing or enhancing any mother-daughter relationship. I highly recommend this book!"

"The Mother Daughter Relationship Makeover by Leslie and Lindsey Glass is a tour de force that every mother and daughter should read to see their own relationship mirrored in the book. with journal suggestions for a path to a happier and healthier relationship."

"Beautifully written and thought provoking. Part autobiographical and part advice, this mother-daughter duo shares their story as well as how you can improve your own mother/daughter relationship."

"Many of us use journaling as a self-reflective tool - writing down our thoughts and feelings to both illuminate and clarify them. The Mother-Daughter Relationship Makeover uses journaling and the authors' powerful, sometimes raw, personal stories as ways to lead you back to the love between mothers and daughters. The anecdotes are personal and powerful. The insights they illuminate are absorbing. I found that many of the accounts paralleled incidents in my relationship with my own mother. I wish she were still here to read this book with me. Highly recommend."

"So much to like about this book - I do journal and this aspect of the book worked well for me. I also, enjoyed the book's overall message. I was a little uncomfortable with the author over sharing but perhaps that is because the experiences of the author were not similar to mine. I did not relate as well as others did."

"The Mother-Daughter Relationship Makeover by Leslie and Lindsey Glass is a heartfelt, transformative journey that offers a powerful blueprint for healing and strengthening the mother-daughter connection. Blending memoir with self-help, Leslie, a bestselling author, and her daughter Lindsey, an award-winning documentarian, bravely share the raw, complex story of their own relationship—one filled with real struggles and reconciliations. This book is a lifeline for mothers and daughters who may feel distanced by conflict, offering a realistic pathway to mending hurt and rediscovering love."

"What sets this book apart is its interactive format. The four-step approach—revealing backstories, exploring emotional styles, understanding conflicts, and learning restorative tools—gives readers a hands-on way to reflect on their own relationships. Through candid storytelling and insightful prompts, Leslie and Lindsey guide readers to new levels of understanding and empathy, showing that no matter the rift, healing is possible."

"What a hopeful message for Mothers and Daughters who feel they are in an irretrievably broken relationship. The Mother-Daughter Relationship Makeover is a masterful exercise to navigate this oftentimes difficult relationship. The journaling prompts at the end of each chapter helped solidify the well thought out lessons within. Leslie and Lindsey's stories were so intimate, exposed and personal that I felt as if I were eavesdropping. However, they showed courage, unwavering determination and commitment to get back to love. All readers can benefit from this book regardless of your Mother/Daughter relationship. Highly recommended."

WHAT PEOPLE ARE SAYING ABOUT LESLIE AND LINDSEY GLASS

Praise for Leslie and Lindsey Glass

"Leslie and Lindsey Glass's new book, The Mother Daughter Relationship Makeover, is certain to make a major contribution to the understanding of what can go wrong, and right, with this most important relationship. Thousands of mothers and daughters wish they could have a relationship like theirs. This high-achieving duo is charming, compassionate, accepting, and open not only with each other but with everyone they touch."
- *Leonard Bushel, author of High: Confessions of a Cannabis Addict and editor/publisher of the Addiction/Recovery e-Bulletin*

"Lindsey and Leslie Glass are incredible resources when it comes to anything recovery related. They have devoted their lives to raising awareness of the many issues regarding addiction, recovery, and prevention. They are talented writers and filmmakers, and have used their talents as recovery advocates to address the stigma that still exists regarding addiction. It's been our pleasure to work with them because they're the genuine article. We wish them continued success, and look forward to any future collaborations."
- *Ken Pomerance, co-founder of InTheRooms.com*

"Lindsey and Leslie Glass have created a wealth of creative and user-friendly recovery and self-help content that inspires thousands of people every single day."
- *Marisa Ravel, owner of Laserkitten*

PRAISE FOR THE SECRET WORLD OF RECOVERY

Amazon reviewers

"Important film! The Secret World Of Recovery is a documentary that anyone dealing with addiction recovery issues should see. Lots of important information about what recovery really means and how people get into long-term sobriety. I recommend this very highly to people who want to know more about dealing with alcoholism and addiction in the family."

"We watch this DVD in our facility. The clients really enjoy it and it makes for quality discussions. The Secret World To Recovery is informative, interesting, and refreshing. The educational pieces are engaging and appropriate for our clients. It is inspiring and it instills hope, laughter, and fun into the hard work of recovery."

"The Secret World of Recovery is a must-see for family members of those struggling with addiction as well as the addict themselves; a good documentary."

PRAISE FOR LINDSEY GLASS'S 100 TIPS FOR GROWING UP

Amazon readers

"100 Tips For Growing Up is beautiful"

"It's simple and relatable"

"It's interactive. I just love the notes to self."

"Recovery content like this is brilliant."

" The tips are easy to digest, and the place for journaling after every tip is a great way to hardwire healthy behaviors into the brain. My patients love it." - *Michael Fitzgerald, director, Acute Care Behavioral Health Program*

PRAISE FOR THE HEALTHY TEEN PROJECT: THE TEEN GUIDE TO HEALTH

From Parents

"Our whole family read the book and will cherish our son's contest experience forever."

"Our son has gained so much confidence from creating art for the mental health contest; he's a different person."

"We learned a lot about anxiety and stress in teens, and our daughter used her project for her college application, and for mentoring students at college when she got in."

From students

"I was surprised by how much I didn't know about mental health. Parents should read it, and teachers too." - *2021 contest winner*

"I learned about brain function and physical health (from the book), made a video about it, entered the contest and won $5,000. It was a joy for my whole family." - *2022 contest winner*

"Doing a project about influences on the teen brain changed my life and habits. Social media is no longer my friend." - *2023 contest winner*

From a participating art teacher

"The hundreds of students who have participated in three years love this book and project. We have few opportunities that provide health education, and none that use art as a stimulus, so this is unique. At the end of the year, families of teens from different schools enjoy seeing the exhibition from other students. The winners will never forget their experience. And having Leslie teach a class brings real excitement to the classroom."

From a participating afterschool program

"Our students are leadership mentors, and this program inspires them to learn more about mental health and what they can do to help others. We have contest winners every year."

PRAISE FOR LESLIE GLASS MYSTERIES

Goodreads reviewers

"Glass delivers what her fans have come to expect – page-turning suspense and dynamic characters... to sum it up in one word: chilling."

"Welcome to Portland... Glas's most provocative character, tracked by the deadliest killers you never want to meet."

PRAISE FOR THE NOVELS OF LESLIE GLASS

"Sharp as a scalpel.. Scary as hell. Leslie Glass is Lady Mcbain." - *Michael Palmer*

"Nobody writes crime mysteries quite like Leslie Glass." - *Romantic Times*

"Brilliant ... skillfully done." - *Tampa Times*

"Truly fantastic." - *New York Post*

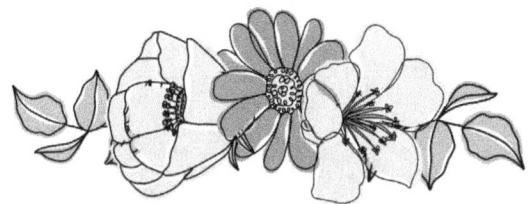

ABOUT THE AUTHORS

Leslie Glass is a journalist, novelist, playwright, and documentarian. In her writing career of more than four decades, she has worked in advertising, publishing, magazines, documentary filmmaking, and theatre. For twenty-four years, she served as Trustee of the **Leslie Glass Family Foundation**, which she retired in 2018. Leslie, has served on many organization boards including, the **Middle States Commission of Higher Education** and the **New York City Police Foundation**. Since 2011, Leslie has concentrated on creating educational tools for life skills, family wellness, and teen addiction prevention. With her daughter Lindsey, she developed the popular website **Reach Out Recovery**, publishing self-help books and more than 1,500 original articles about addiction, recovery, and family relationships. Leslie is also the author of fourteen novels, including nine **USA Today** and **New York Times** bestselling crime novels featuring NYPD Detective Sergeant April Woo, the first female Asian-American detective in main-stream American fiction. Leslie lives in Sarasota, Florida, where her passions are Tai Chi, golf, cooking for friends and neighbors, and the **Rotary Club of Sarasota Bay**, where she developed the "What Makes You Healthy" wellness education and art program for teens based on her book, **The Teen Guide To Health.**

Lindsey Glass is an author, screenwriter, and recovery/mental health advocate. She has worked in publishing and film as well as in the non-profit world for over two decades. She has coproduced two documentaries on addiction recovery and teen empowerment and is cofounder of the popular wellness website **Reach Out Recovery.** Lindsey has written dozens of articles about recovery, relationships, and wellness that have been read millions of times worldwide. A passionate advocate for those suffering with addiction and mental health issues, Lindsey is the president of **ROR Empowerment,** the non-profit arm of Reach Out Recovery. Since 2012, Lindsey has worked tirelessly to develop tools and provide access to information about recovery and emotional wellness including programs, books, workbooks, and curriculums. Lindsey cares deeply about social issues, She lives in Sarasota, Florida and is a passionate dog enthusiast.